D0290459

HONOR AND SHAME

3539-GIBS

HONOR AND SHAME

Unlocking the Door

Roland Muller

3539-GIBS

Copyright © 2000 by Roland Muller.

ISBN #:   Softcover   0-7388-4316-4

All rights reserved. No part of this book may be reproduced or transmitted in any form or by any means, electronic or mechanical, including photocopying, recording, or by any information storage and retrieval system, without permission in writing from the copyright owner.

This book was printed in the United States of America.

To order additional copies of this book, contact:
Xlibris Corporation
1-888-7-XLIBRIS
www.Xlibris.com
Orders@Xlibris.com

CONTENTS

Unless otherwise indicated, all scriptures are taken from the
HOLY BIBLE, NEW INTERNATIONAL VERSION.
Copyright 1973,1978,1984, by International Bible Soci-
ety. Used by permission of Zondervan Publishing House.
All rights reserved.

The "NIV" and "New International Version" trademarks
are registered in the United States Patent and Trademark
Office by International Bible Society. Use of either trademark requires the permission of International Bible Society.

3539-GIBS

ACKNOWLEDGMENTS

People are usually better resources than books. They are more current, personal, and can usually answer questions when posed to them. In the back of this book is a bibliography of the related books that I have read. But this list pales in significance when I think of the many people I have interacted with, and learned from, as I researched the topics in this book.

So in the beginning, I would like to acknowledge the many brothers and sisters laboring in the Muslim world who have shared with me their struggle to communicate Christ's grace with those from a Muslim heritage. I would also like to thank all the missionaries, missiologists, and theologians who have given me suggestions. So many things that were shared, became part of the catalyst that created the thinking in this book.

Special thanks, however, must go to Ken Betts, a close friend, who spent many hours with me, talking through the issues that became fundamental to this book. Along with this he shared his own personal journey into the world of honor and shame. Without his insight and encouragement, this book might never have been written. Others, like Dr. Mazen Hanna and Dr. George Kelsey, must also be thanked for the time they gave and for all of the insights they shared from their own Middle Eastern experience.

Lastly, Bryan Wylie must be thanked for the time he put into checking manuscripts and correcting my grammar. Without his help, this manuscript might never have made it to print.

Roland Muller

Other books by Roland Muller
- The Man from Gadara
- Tools for Muslim Evangelism
- Missionary Leadership, by Motivation and Communication

INTRODUCTION

Every individual is different. He or she is a unique mixture of person, personality, culture, and background. I strongly believe that there is no such thing as a generic key that will unlock the spiritual door to every person's life. Any missionary who dreams of doing *the magic thing*, or saying the magic words, that will suddenly open the eyes of an individual to the truth of the gospel, is merely dreaming of a way to avoid the hard work of understanding, empathizing and effectively communicating the gospel to an individual.

There are, however, special keys that we must hold and exercise, if we are to do this work of understanding, empathizing and communicating to different people in different cultures. During my missionary career, I have focused my attention on understanding and communicating the gospel to the Muslim people of the Middle East. In the past, many Christian scholars and missionaries have sought answers to Islam, through the very form of Islam itself. They have sought to correct Muslim misunderstandings, develop redemptive analogies, and inform the Christian public at large about the intricacies of the Islamic religion. Missionaries have gone the extra mile in studying Islamic religion and history, and many have attempted to remove the barriers of culture by contextualizing themselves into some form of Christian that Muslims can understand. And yet we still seek for a workable solution . . . that mystical, magical something that will touch the Islamic world so they can see and understand who Christ is.

I am very much aware that I have more questions than answers, but, during these last few years, I have become increasingly aware of the importance of communicating through culture. We westerners have tended to divide people into two sections. We look at their religious beliefs separately from their cultural ones. When we come to Muslims, we tend to draw out verses from the Qur'an and the Hadith on God, sin and salvation. From these verses we try to develop an Islamic theology that we can understand. In the process of doing this, we often disregard verses that deal with cultural issues, such as women, relationships, and the community. We do this, because we are used to doing this in our western religious setting. We call it separation of church and state. Second, we also understand that new communities of believers are free to contextualize the gospel into their own cultural setting. So, when we approach Islam, we tend to separate cultural and religious teachings and concentrate on confronting the religious issues and then adopting as much of the culture as possible. To the Muslim, who sees Islam and Islamic culture as a total package, we must appear to be very confused and confusing.

In this book, I would like to draw your attention to the Gospel message that we are trying to communicate. Does it address the worldview and specific culture that we are facing? In the case of Islam, our message must include both religious and cultural issues if we are to minister the gospel effectively to Muslims. I am convinced that it is not the religious side of Islam that holds its followers in an iron grip, but rather the cultural and the community side. Yet, even here we must be careful, for Islam is not made up of two sides, or three sides, or whatever. It is a complete unit, a way of life, a total package that touches every part of life.

Ministering the gospel to people whose lives are dominated by Islam is never easy. In "Tools for Muslim Evangelism" I introduced the concept of 'teacher-based' evangelism and explored how this form of evangelism has been instrumental in bringing many Muslims to Christ. I then went on to mention the concepts of honor and trust and explored some of the implications of sharing the Gospel with people who place honor high on their value list.

In the book you now hold in your hands, we will take the concept of honor and dig even deeper, introducing the idea of honor and shame as a basis for Islamic culture. We will compare it to guilt and innocence which is the basis of many western cultures, and fear and power, which is the basis of many animistic cultures. The ultimate goal in this book is to provide basic concepts and tools for those wishing to share the gospel with their Muslim neighbors. My desire is not to change the gospel message but, rather, to provide the Christian teacher with concepts and tools that will better enable him or her to understand the Muslims they are trying to reach, and know how to make the gospel relevant to their world view.

May God bless you as you read through these pages, and may He give you the wisdom you need to discover what is relevant to the people God has placed in your path, so you may share the message of God's grace with them.

Roland Muller

CHAPTER ONE

The Eden Effect

The only reason that the missionary enterprise exists today is because sin exists. Sin began in the Garden of Eden and has affected mankind ever since. The missionary enterprise of the church exists simply for the purpose of addressing sin and the results of sin, among the peoples of the earth; communicating to people everywhere the gospel of God's grace provided through the cross of Christ. In the medical world, if there was no such thing as disease and if everyone was healthy, then there would be no need for the entire health care industry. In the same way, if sin ceased to exist, then there would be no need for the entire missionary enterprise.

Since the missionary effort is so closely attached to sin, I believe it is important for us to have a very clear understanding of how sin entered the world, and the immediate impact that that sin had on the human race. As mankind multiplied on the face of the earth, sin multiplied, until today we have a world full of people, and thus a world full of sin and the results of sin. If we can understand the significance of what took place in the Garden of Eden, I believe we can begin to understand the peoples of the world today, in their various lifestyles as they try to cope with sin and the influences of sin in their communities.

So, whenever we set out to understand the mindset of a certain culture or worldview, we need to start in the Bible, with the Garden of Eden. It is my belief that if we can understand man in the Garden of Eden, then we can begin to understand how man's thinking has developed in different directions from that point.

In Genesis 3 we find that man is influenced in three ways as a result of sin. There are also a number of consequences from this sin, but we want to examine the three basic influences sin has on man.

Over time, these three basic influences have become the building blocks of worldview. And, if the Bible is what it says it is, (i.e. God's communication to mankind in every place,) then the Gospel message in the Bible should address each of these basic building blocks, and speak specifically to them.

We must be careful, however, not to try and fit each culture or worldview into one specific category. These building blocks are similar to an artist, creating thousands of colours from three basic primary colors. How much of each primary color is used, determines what the final color will be when the paint is mixed. In the same way, all three building blocks are present in all cultures and worldviews, but how much of each one is present, determines the actual type of culture that emerges.

Having determined this, one must also consider how people in a particular local culture react to the elements of the overall culture. As an example, when an Arab is shamed, he may react by killing the one who causes the shame, but when an oriental is shamed, he may react by committing suicide. But first, lets examine the three basic building blocks as found in the Garden of Eden.

The Influence of Sin

We know very little about man's original state. The first two chapters of Genesis describe to us a world before it was tainted with sin. Likewise, the last two chapters of Revelation describe to us a world that has been totally freed of sin. Everything in between has to do with a world that has been affected by sin. However, from the first two chapters of Genesis we know that mankind was created in the image of God, and that he had dominion over the earth. Lots of people have speculated about man's original condition, but the fact is that there is very little information available.

We do, however, know a great deal about man's condition after the fall, as all of us live in this condition. But while we live under the effects of the fall, we may never have taken time to study those effects and how they affect our lives today.

The Bible points out that there were three specific effects to Adam and Eve's sin in the garden. These three effects are the three basic emotional reactions to sin, and are found in Genesis chapter 3. In verse seven, the Bible tells us that Adam and Eve knew that they were naked, and they sewed fig leaves together to make an apron. This knowledge of sin is nothing other than the feeling of guilt. When Adam and Eve sinned, their consciences kicked in and immediately they felt guilt. They immediately knew they had done wrong. This knowledge of good and evil is common to us today. While Adam and Eve were in their perfect state, they had never felt their consciences condemning them. As soon as they sinned, they felt the sting of their conscience, and they knew right from wrong.

The problem with conscience is that conscience can be silenced after a time. However, even if this is the case, and conscience is no longer operating, this does not mean that people are not guilty. When Adam sinned, he was not only guilty of eating forbidden fruit, but in that one act, guilt passed upon all of mankind, forever.

All of this, of course, is familiar territory for most Christians. Every western book on Christian theology examines man's guilt, which originated in the Garden of Eden. Guilt is then traced through the Bible, and verses are drawn out where God addresses guilt in the Old and New Testament. Theologians are quick to point out the meaning of the scapegoat in Leviticus, the guilt offerings and so forth.

This is all good and proper, but unfortunately, many Christians, and some Christian theology, stop with guilt, or rather, get so wrapped up with 'guilt-based theology' that they fail to notice the other influences of sin.

Our attraction to the guilt aspect of the fall and consequently the guilt aspect of salvation is due in part to our preoccupation with guilt as a western culture. Much of the English speaking world and parts of Europe have worldviews that focus in on the aspect of man's guilt, and/or his freedom from guilt. This is what I will call in this book *"guilt-based culture."* In chapters two, three and four we will examine guilt-based cultures, how they came into being, and the impact these have had on our western Christian theology.

Guilt, however, was not the only influence of sin in the Garden of Eden. When Adam and Eve realized they had sinned, they immediately hid themselves (v. 8). Adam and Eve were ashamed. Shame had come upon Adam and Eve, but their shame was not only for them alone. Shame, like guilt, passed upon all of mankind from that point on. As a result, Man is not only guilty from this point on, but man is also in a position of shame before God.

It is interesting to note that the subject of shame is addressed in the Old Testament. You can find references to it in the imagery of the temple, in the messages of the prophets, and, more importantly, in the death of Christ on the cross. Shame is repeatedly mentioned in the New Testament, especially in the teachings of Christ in the Gospels.

Anthropologists and sociologists have pointed out to us that many cultures around the world focus in on the aspects of shame and honor, rather than guilt and innocence. Honor and shame are paramount to understanding their worldviews. The shame-based cultures of the world span an area from Morocco to Korea, and cover much of what is known today in mission circles as the 10/40 window. They also exist among the aboriginal natives of North America.

In this book we will look at shame-based cultures in chapters six, seven and eight, and at the relationship between Islam and shame-based cultures in chapters nine and ten.

Guilt and shame, however, were not the only influences of sin. When God came to speak to Adam and Eve in the garden, Adam told God that they had hid themselves because they were afraid (v 10). The third influence of sin was fear, and fear came upon Adam and Eve, and also upon the whole human race. Before this, man enjoyed the presence of God. Now he cowered in fear, and fear passed upon all of mankind from that point on. Many books about Christian theology seem to miss this point even though missionaries have long talked about fear-based cultures that exist among animistic people.

From Genesis 3 we see that man is not only in a position of guilt and shame, but man is also in a position of fear before God. Moreover, it is interesting to note that the subject of fear is addressed in the Old Testament. You can find it in the imagery of the temple, in the messages of the prophets, and more importantly in the Garden of Gethsemane before the death of Christ. The New Testament also repeatedly addresses the issue of fear. (e.g. "For you did not receive a spirit that makes you a slave again to fear but you received the Spirit of sonship." Romans 8:15 and "There is no fear in love, but perfect love drives out all fear." I John 4:18)

Anthropologists and sociologists tell us that many cultures in our world are fear-based cultures. These cultures focus in on fear of spirits and the supernatural world. The aspect of fear is paramount to understanding their worldview. Fear-based cultures are found in Africa, Central and South America, and some islands in the Far East. In this book we will look at fear-based cultures in chapter five.

The Development of Three Great Worldviews

Down through history and across the world, these three emotional reactions to sin became the three basic building blocks that exist in all cultures today. Some cultures have more of one than another, but all three are present in all cultures today.

Furthermore, there are great areas of the world that have similar cultures, while other locations have such a mix of the three that it is hard to classify them.

Where are the major blocks? Many western nations (Northern Europe, North America, Australia and New Zealand) have cultures that contain mostly guilt-based cultural characteristics. On the other hand, much of the 10/40 window is made up shame-based cultures. Most of the primal religions and cultures of the world (such as tribes in the jungles of Africa, Asia and South America) are structured around fear-based principles.

The problem comes when we want to simply classify cultures into these three basic classifications. They do not easily fit, because they are made up of blends of all three.

Thus, when analyzing a culture, one must look for the primary cultural characteristics, and then the secondary ones. As an example, many North American Native cultures are made up of elements of both shame-based and fear-based cultures. On the other hand, much of North American culture has been made up almost exclusively of guilt-based principles, although this has changed in the last two decades.

Missionary Efforts in the Past

During the history of missions, the church has done well among some cultures and has related poorly to others. As missionaries have entered cultures that are built on the principles of fear, they have done well, presenting Christ's work on the cross as providing victory over the spirit world.

In the shame-based cultures of the 10/40 window, we have done much poorer. Where there has been a blend of shame and fear-based cultures, the church has done reasonably well, but in the Muslim cultures of the Middle East, which are primarily shame-based, the church has struggled to communicate the gospel in an effective manner.

I have been greatly encouraged, as I have observed missionaries using principles from this book. For many of them it has unlocked the door, so that they could further explore the richness of God's grace as it has been poured out for those from a shame-based culture just as it had been poured out for those from guilt and fear-based cultures.

Conclusion

When man sinned, three great conditions came upon mankind. When man broke God's law, he was in a position of guilt. When man broke God's relationship, he was in a position of shame. When man broke God's trust, he was in a position of fear.

As cultures and worldviews developed over the millennia that followed, they have gravitated towards one of these conditions. This polarization has created these three mega-trends in worldview. While the majority of worldviews fits into these three classifications, many cultures draw equally from two or all three worldviews.

This mixing of worldviews is especially noticeable in South America where jungle tribes with fear-based cultures come in contact with shame-based cultures originating out of southern Spain, and guilt-based cultures brought by western missionaries and western business. The goal of this book is to simply introduce the idea of guilt, shame and fear based cultures, and then to examine how the gospel is best communicated in it's entirety. My case study in how this might be done is based on my experiences in the shame-based Islamic cultures of the Middle East.

In order for us to examine these three worldviews, I have started with a frank look at our western guilt-based cultures. This is the basis for the culture that I was born in, and one that I claim as my own. My study of how this worldview has developed has helped me understand my own culture. This understanding is important if we are to move on and attempt to understand how other cultures think.

CHAPTER TWO

Guilt-Based Culture

None of us lives in exactly the same culture. Culture varies from town to town, family to family and sometimes even from individual to individual. All of us are different. We are made up of different fabrics and formed by the different experiences that come into our lives on a day to day basis. Even those who try to define "American" or "Canadian" culture can only talk in vague generalizations. "Americans" come from all kinds of ethnic backgrounds, and have all kinds of values. Some live in middle class housing, some in cardboard boxes on the street, and some in large impressive mansions. It's hard to place categorizations and descriptions on people who are so diverse.

Despite this, however, there are some general characteristics or mega-traits that fit the majority of people in our "western population." Certain basic fundamental beliefs have molded our western civilization. These beliefs have laid the foundations upon which our nations are built, and from which the fabric of our society has been formed.

One of these basic foundations is our belief in right versus wrong. This understanding is so deeply ingrained in our western culture, that we analyze almost everything from this perspective. Most of our forms of entertainment are built upon 'the good guys and the bad guys.' It is so familiar to us, that few of us question its validity. It is such an integral part of our religion and society, that we often cannot imagine a world where 'right versus wrong' isn't the accepted basic underlying principle.

Right versus wrong is the yardstick we use in our culture with which to measure everything else with. We talk about the rightness and wrongness of someone else's actions. We talk about things being "right for me." We are obsessed with knowing our rights and exercising them. Our society spends countless hours and billions of dollars debating the wrongs of society. Is homosexuality right or wrong? Is spending billions on the military right or wrong? Is possession of drugs right or wrong? How about possession of nuclear bombs, or weapons of mass destruction?

Almost every major issue the west struggles with, involves an aspect of deciding whether something is right or wrong. We arrive at this basic tension in life because almost everything in our culture is plotted between guilt and innocence. (Innocence being something we define as being right or righteousness).

The pulls and demands of these two diametrically opposed forces dictate much of our western human behavior. Guilt can plague and haunt us bringing fear and condemnation upon us. We do everything we can to avoid being guilty. Psychologists spend a great deal of their time helping people deal with all sorts of guilt complexes.

Evangelicals in particular, often live in circles that are governed by guilt principles based on the authority of the Bible. Outside of these circles, guilt is defined in many ways. It can be a sense of public disapproval, being in trouble with the authorities, or not being politically correct. However guilt is defined, and to what extent it influences a culture vary widely from location to location. However, our understanding of right and wrong has been instrumental in forming much of western society.

On the other end of the spectrum, is righteousness, or innocence. This is the unspoken goal of our society. "I'm OK, you're OK" is the most comfortable situation for us. All of us want to express our innocence with the statement that we are as good as the next guy. If this is true, then we can get about our business of pursuing happiness and pleasure within the bounds of being OK and not guilty.

Most of us do what we can to avoid being guilty and at the same time exercise our rights. This guilt/innocence thinking is so ingrained in our society that most of us have immediate reflexes to events that catch us off guard.

Have you ever noticed what happens in the swimming pool when the lifeguard blows his whistle? We stop to see who is guilty, and when we realize we are innocent we resume swimming. This is a normal scenario from the western world, but it is not true of the Muslim world. When we in the western world do something wrong, like unintentionally running a red light, we may feel guilty. This is not necessarily true in the Muslim world.

Or, how about this? Imagine a classroom full of grade school kids. Suddenly, the intercom interrupts their class. Johnny is being called to the principle's office. What is the immediate reaction of the other children? "What did you do wrong?" they ask. Even our children immediately assume guilt. Perhaps the school principal is going to hand out rewards, but our society conditions us to expect the worst, and we feel pangs of guilt.

When trying to share the gospel with people in our western culture, we usually start from the premise of guilt, as taught in Romans 3. All are guilty of breaking God's law. I've noticed an immediate reaction to these feelings of guilt on many people's behalf. "Well, I think I'm as good as the next fellow" or "I'll take my chances." Even people on the street immediately associate the Christian religion with guilt. A mosque in Canada once displayed a sign: "We accept everyone, and tell no one that he is a sinner."

So much of our western thinking is wrapped up in guilt. Wars are justified on the basis of establishing guilt. During the opening days of the Gulf War, the American government spent many hours and millions of dollars determining if Saddam Hussein was guilty. Once they established that he was guilty of committing atrocities they had the right to take military action against him. Throughout the war, they continued to make statements about Mr. Hussein's deranged mental state and irrational actions. All of this helped justify the war. In fact, all during the history of western civilizations, wars have had to be justified, and each side identifies the other as being the 'bad guys.'

But some things are not easy to chart between right and wrong. Is a hungry child stealing food guilty? Should he be punished despite his hunger? These questions disturb us, because we feel that everything in life must fit somewhere between guilt and innocence.

In fact, our association with guilt has gone so far as to provide an avenue for people to develop guilt complexes. They feel guilt for what they have done and also guilt for what they have not done. They even feel guilt for what others have done. People who struggle with a guilt complex can even be overcome with embarrassment and feelings of guilt from the actions of others.

The flip side of guilt is innocence, righteousness, and exercising rights. As I mentioned, "I'm OK, you're OK" is an important philosophy in our culture. In order not to point our finger at people, we continue to expand the limits of what is acceptable activity. By making homosexuality acceptable, we help thousands of people avoid feeling guilty. This alone is enough to convince many people in our society that it's OK for people to be homosexual. In fact, almost anything is tolerated as long as it doesn't hurt another person.

I have been surprised to discover that many people in our western world believe that our fixation with right and wrong is not only normal, but also the only correct way to think. They assume that anyone, who does not think in these terms, does not think rationally or logically.

Furthermore, there are many Christians who believe that a culture that is based on right and wrong is based on Judeo-Christian principles and therefore is correct. I've noticed time and time again that this objection is quickly withdrawn as we look into the origins of our guilt-based culture, and ask ourselves honestly, if this is the only valid pattern set down in the scriptures.

In order to understand our guilt-based culture, we must go back to Greek and Roman times, and examine the origin of this pattern of thinking, and discover how this has had an impact on the church, and on our understanding of the scriptures.

CHAPTER THREE

The Roman Connection

The Roman Empire has come and gone, leaving us with a few ruined cities, and a wealth of stories about conquest and heroism. While most of what the Romans accomplished has disappeared, there is one facet of Roman life that has impacted the west, right down to the present. It is the Roman law, or the *'pax romana'* (Roman peace) which was brought about by everyone obeying the Roman law.

Roman law introduced us to the concept that the law was above everyone, even the lawmakers. This idea was not new. The Jews under Moses understood this. Greek politicians developed a similar plan, but with laws that were man made, not divine. The Romans, however, perfected the system, and put it into widespread use. They developed a type of democracy known as the republic. They put in place a complex legal system that required lawmakers, lawyers, and judges. This Roman system of law left a tremendous impact on our society. Even to this day, much of our own legal system is still built around the basic Roman code of law.

Western civilization today is littered with references to the Roman Empire. Much of our coins, architecture, and language have Roman roots. Our legal and economic theories are so filled with Romanisms that we no longer see them for what they are. They have become so much a part of our mental furniture, that few people today question them. As an example, Roman Law during the Roman Empire assumed that the individual's rights were granted by the state (by government) and that lawmakers can make up laws. Under Roman law, the state was supreme, and rights were granted or erased whenever lawmakers decided. This philosophy is sometimes called 'statism.' Its basic premise is that there is no law higher than the government's law.

Roman politicians were not the first to invent statism but they did such an effective job of applying it, that the Roman Empire has become the guiding star for politicians everywhere. Statists see the "*pax romana*," the period in which Rome dominated the Mediterranean world, as the golden days of statism. The known world was "unified" and controlled by one large government. This unification was symbolized in Roman times by something known as the *fasces*. This was a bundle of wooden rods bound together by red-colored bands. In ancient Rome the fasces was fixed to a wooden pole, with an ax at the top or side. This symbolized the unification of the people under a single government. The ax suggested what would happen to anyone who didn't obey the government. The Roman fasces is the origin of the word *fascism*.

During Roman times, *pax romana* (the Roman peace) meant, "do as you are told, don't make waves, or you will be hauled away in chains." Roman Law was supreme. In contrast to this, there was the old way of obeying the supreme ruler. Under this system, the word of the ruler was law. With the Republic, the Romans elevated law, so that it was above the ruler. Now everyone, even the emperor of Rome had to obey the law. The law, not the ruler determined if people were innocent or guilty.

It is interesting to note, that as the early church developed and grew, Roman law also had an impact on Christian theology. Since Roman law interpreted everything in the terms of right versus wrong, early Christians were deeply influenced by this thinking.

Early Church Theologians

Tertullian, the early church father who first developed a code of systematic theology, was a lawyer steeped in Roman law. Using his understanding of law, and the need for justice, guilt, and redemption, he laid the basis for Christian systematic theology, as it would develop in the west.

Tertullian was born shortly before 160 AD, into the home of a Roman centurion on duty in Carthage. He was trained in both Greek and Latin, and was very much at home in the classics. He became a proficient Roman lawyer and taught public speaking and practiced law in Rome, where he was converted to Christianity. In the years that followed he became the outstanding apologist of the Western Church and the first known author of Christian systematic theology.

Basil the Great was born in 329 AD, and after completing his education in Athens he went on to practice law and teach rhetoric. In 370 AD, Basil, the lawyer, became Basil the Bishop when he was elected bishop of Caesarea. During his time as Bishop he wrote many books in defense of the deity of Christ and of the Holy Spirit. Basil's training in law and rhetoric gave him the tools he needed to speak out in defense of the church.

Next came **Augustine** who was born in 354 AD into the home of a Roman official in the North African town of Tagaste. He received his early education in the local school, where he learned Latin to the accompaniment of many beatings. He hated studying the Greek language so much that he never learned to use it proficiently. He was sent to school in nearby Madaura and from there went to Carthage to study rhetoric, a technique used in Roman law for debate. He then taught legal rhetoric in his hometown and Carthage until he went to Milan in 384 AD. He was converted in 386 and became a priest in 391. He returned to Africa and became a prolific writer and bishop. No other Christian after Paul has had such a wide and deep impact on the Christian world through his writings as Augustine.

Ambrose was born around 340 AD, in Gaul. When his father, the prefect of Gaul, died, the family moved to Rome where Ambrose was educated for the legal profession. Later, he was appointed civil governor over a large territory, being headquartered in Milan. Upon the death of the bishop of Milan in 374, the people unanimously wanted him to take that position. Believing this to be the call of God, he gave up his high political position, distributed his money to the poor, and became a bishop. In 374, Ambrose demonstrated his ability in the fields of church administration, preaching, and theology. But as always, his training in Roman law enforced his views of guilt and righteousness.

Have you noticed the impact that law and lawyers had on the development of the early church? This trend did not stop with the early church.

Reformation Theologians

John Calvin was born in 1505 in northeastern France where his father was a respected citizen. He studied Humanistic Studies at the University of Paris, and then law at the University of Orleans, and finally at the University of Bourges. Sometime between 1532 and 1533 he converted and adopted the ideas of the reformation. The writings of John Calvin, the lawyer and theologian, have had a tremendous impact on our society.

Calvin was not alone. Others, like **Arnauld Antoine** the French theologian (1612-1694), studied at Calvi and Lisieux, first law, then theology. He was made a priest and doctor in 1634. Arnauld spoke out against the Jesuits and his writings added to the impact of the reformation.

There are more examples of theologians who were also lawyers, but this list will suffice to point out that legal thought and expression had much to do with the development of the theology of the Early Church. Each of these church leaders continued to develop the relationship between Christianity, as it was known in the west, and the legal understanding of guilt, justice, and righteousness. These lawyers were concerned with establishing guilt, or innocence, and they brought this emphasis with them, into their theology. And we, the western church, have used their theology to build our civilizations.

In the ensuing years, new nations in the New World would be founded on the theological basis developed by these church leaders. The United States of America was founded on these principles. The American founders attempted to establish a nation built on the Roman principle of a republic, and on the early church's understanding of right and wrong.

Today, it is interesting to notice that some non-western sources link guilt-based culture with Christianity. In October 1999, Isaiah Kalinowski, the Opinion Editor for the Jordan Times, wrote an article entitled "The Shame Culture that is Wabash." In this article he pointed out: ". . . *guilt culture is due largely to Christianity. A shame culture is one in which individuals are kept from transgressing the social order by fear of public disgrace. On the other hand, in a guilt culture, one's own moral attitudes and fear of retribution in the distant future are what enforce the ethical behavior of a member of that society.*"

From Kalinowski's perspective, guilt-based culture is linked to Christian theology. This is an unfortunate misrepresentation, as the Bible speaks to all cultures and worldviews (as we will see later in this book.) On the other hand, we, as Christians, must recognize the incredible impact that guilt-based culture has had on our understanding and interpretation of the Bible in the Christian west.

The Eastern Scene

Christianity in the east, however, developed differently. Eastern theologians did not use Roman law as a vehicle for interpreting the gospel. Rather, the eastern world was caught up in the shame-honor relationship that was prevalent in societies scattered from the Middle East to the Far East. Eastern Orthodox theology didn't deal directly with sin, guilt, and redemption. They dealt more with the issue of us being able to stand in the presence of God or not, and in our relationship with God, and with others around us.

Chrysostom, the early church theologian for the Eastern Church, was born about 345 AD into a wealthy aristocratic family in Antioch. He was a student of the sophist Libanius who had been a friend of the Emperor Julian. This man gave him a good training in the Greek classics and rhetoric that laid the foundation for his excellent speaking ability. After his baptism in 368, he became a monk in the eastern churches. Chrysostom rose to being an outstanding preacher, even winning the acclaim of the emperor. Today we have a record of around 680 of Chrystostom's sermons and homilies and I am told that he never once preached on justification. In the end, he was banished because he spoke out so sharply against the views of the western theologians.

Islam

In the same way, Islam, which rose to prominence around 600 AD, teaches that God remains over all, and that law is in his hands, not the hands of lawmakers.

The Qur'an enforces the principle that God is overall with the story about Pharaoh and how he was shown Allah's *"mightiest miracle, but he denied it and rebelled. The Pharaoh quickly went away and summoning all his men, made to them a proclamation. 'I am your supreme Lord.* The Qur'an then tells us that Allah *"Smote him,"* and goes on to warn, *"Surely in this there is a lesson for the God fearing."*

Therefore it would be unthinkable to a Muslim, that a lawmaker could make a law that is over all. This is why Islam presents both a religious and a cultural pattern for people to live by. God dictates both moral laws and civil laws.

Conclusion

It is important to realize that, as Christians, we must carefully examine our Biblical perspectives. Certain passages of Scripture are very meaningful to us because they speak to our own worldview, but they may not be as meaningful to people from other worldviews. When explaining the gospel, we often find Paul's letter to the Romans useful. However, we must think carefully about who Paul intended his audience to be. Paul was writing to people living in Rome under Roman law. If Paul contextualized his message to the Greeks at Mars Hill as recorded in Acts 17:16-34, there is no reason to think that he is not contextualizing his message to the Romans who lived under Roman Law.

And so, as westerners living in a culture that has been greatly influenced by guilt-based culture, we usually find our Biblical explanation of the gospel in Paul's letter to the Romans. In fact, when pressed, most western believers have a hard time finding the gospel in the Gospels. There is nothing wrong with this. We in the west live under governments patterned after the Roman form of government. Our thinking and our theology is very Roman in nature, and it is only natural that we will be drawn to Paul's letter to the Romans to find an explanation of the Gospel that is meaningful to us.

I was once asked, when presenting this material, if I was saying that evangelical theology is wrong. I had to smile at this, as I realized that my listener was trying to fit the material I was presenting on a plane between right and wrong. It sounded like I was criticizing our Christian heritage and interpretation of the Bible, and thus, saying that our theology in the west was wrong. This is not the case. I am merely pointing out that our understanding of the gospel, and the Bible verses we find meaningful to us, is influenced by our history and our worldview.

The danger comes, however, when we take our Roman understanding of the Gospel and apply it to those who do not have a Roman-based culture. We fruitlessly spend untold hours and incalculable amounts of energy explaining to our contact that he is guilty of sin, and needs to be justified before God. The poor person, on the other hand, may not even have a word for sin, or perhaps even the concept of sin, in his language. He struggles to understand guilt, and sees no need for justification.

When he doesn't respond, we label him as resistant. We feel good about having given the gospel, because we analyze our own efforts by the measuring stick of right and wrong, and if we did all the right things, and he did not respond, then he must be resistant.

The answer to this dilemma is quite simple. We must put our Roman, guilt-based understanding of the gospel aside, and strive to understand other worldviews and their thinking. Then we need to return to the Bible and discover a way of communicating the gospel to a mindset that is not pre-occupied with right and wrong, or guilt and innocence. God's grace is equally applicable to every society and every culture. It is the duty of the cross-cultural communicator to discover exactly how he or she can best communicate the gospel so that others can understand God's grace offered to mankind in their own culture. I trust that the materials in this book will open the door and start missionaries down this path, if they aren't on it already.

CHAPTER FOUR

The Legal Model of Salvation

The missionary's taxi screeched to a halt. Lying in the middle of the street was a teen-age girl, dying. She had been shot in the head four times. Just then her brother walked across the street with two policemen and stated, "There she is. I killed her because she was in an immoral situation with a man." Under the laws of the country, the young man was innocent. He had not committed murder but had preserved the honor of his family.

In another case, a girl ran away from home. Later her family learned she had married someone from another religion. They were furious. The police imprisoned the girl so that she would be protected from her family. Elderly grandmothers taunted the brother and father. "How long do we need to keep our heads to the ground in shame? Won't you do something to cleanse the shame from our tribe so we can raise our heads and live in honor once again?" The family finally agreed to pay the police a $50,000.00 guarantee that they would not hurt her and she was released into their custody. Within hours her father and brother shot her thirteen times. The entire family was pleased that honor had been restored.

When faced with such situations, many missionaries are exasperated. The cultures that they are living in seem to have no sense of right and wrong. If people don't feel they have broken God's law, then there is no need for salvation or a savior. Christ's death on the cross seems futile and meaningless. The western evangelist, locked into his legal model of salvation, seems powerless to adequately explain the gospel so that people will respond.

We in the west have perfected our legal view of salvation. In saying this, I am not saying that we have entered into legalism, but rather that we usually express the gospel message only in legal thought and terminology. We talk about guilt and the need for redemption. We talk about breaking God's laws, and being under condemnation. These are all legal (and biblical) concepts.

Expressing our salvation in legal terminology is not wrong. It is perfectly acceptable to draw out of Scriptures the legal references to salvation and express God's plan of salvation through them. Not only is it acceptable, it is preferred, for those who live in a world that functions within legal paradigms.

Western church historians, from Tertullian to today, have worked hard at expressing theological concepts in a way that relates to our culture. This is important. But the legal view of salvation is not necessarily the only view of salvation.

In the west we have developed two popular methods of sharing the gospel. These methods are useful when sharing the gospel with people from guilt-based cultures. However, since they draw almost exclusively on legal concepts, they are difficult, if not impossible for those living in a shame-based culture to understand.

Method One: *The Romans Road*

Step One: All are guilty and we must admit we are guilty sinners. Romans 3:10 and Romans 3:23

Step Two: God's penalty for sin is death. Romans 6:23

Step Three: A person can escape God's wrath, by saying a simple prayer, and believing in his heart. Romans 10:9 and Romans 10:13

This plan of salvation is very legal. It doesn't require much knowledge, other than accepting the fact that we are guilty and that God offers us pardon. This approach seems to work well in our western setting, because most people are aware of the concept of guilt. Because of our cultural conditioning, people often feel guilt about something already, and an explanation of how God can remove man's guilt appeals to a felt need in our society. The limitations of this approach are that it requires the hearer to have an understanding of the concept of sin and guilt and secondly, that it stops at the cross. There is little in *The Romans Road* to address the issues and problems that the believer will have after he confesses and believes.

Method Two: *The Four Spiritual Laws*

This approach teaches us that just as there are physical laws that govern the physical universe, so there are spiritual laws, which govern your relationship with God.

Law One: God loves you, and offers a wonderful plan for your life. John 3:16, John 10:10

Law Two: Man is sinful and separated from God. Therefore he cannot know and experience God's love and plan for his life Romans 3:23. Man was created to have fellowship with God; but, because of his stubborn self-will, he chose to go his own independent way and fellowship with God was broken. This self-will, characterized by an attitude of active rebellion or passive indifference, is evidence of what the Bible calls sin. Romans 6:23 God is holy and man is sinful. A great gulf separates the two: Man is continually trying to reach God and the abundant life through his own efforts, such as a good life, philosophy or religion.

Law Three: Jesus Christ is God's only provision for man's sin. Through him you can know and experience God's love and plan for your life. Romans 5:8, I Corinthians 15:3-6, John 14:6. God has bridged the gulf, which separates us from God by sending His Son, Jesus Christ, to die on the cross in our place to pay the penalty for our sins.

Law Four: We must individually receive Jesus Christ as Savior and Lord; then we can know and experience God's love and plan for our lives. John 1:12, Ephesians 2:8,9, John 3:1-8, Revelation 3:20.

Once again, this explanation of the gospel appeals to our guilt-based culture. Even the name: *Four Spiritual Laws* appeals to our understanding of guilt and innocence. This plan, like *The Romans Road* has severe limitations for those in a shame-based culture. It requires an understanding of the concept of sin, and it fails to address the life of the believer after he confesses and believes.

These explanations of the gospel work in the west because most people understand the concept of there being higher laws, and the concept of sin and guilt. Secondly, most people in our society live with a certain measure of guilt, and these two methods of expressing the gospel help people deal with their guilt.

Also, as a church we have augmented these methods of sharing the gospel with other avenues of teaching. We expect that the new believer will take discipleship lessons so he can grow spiritually, and we expect the new believer should regularly attend a church where he or she can gain from the teaching and the fellowship. All of this should help the new believer grasp a fuller understanding of what the gospel is all about.

As one carefully considers these explanations of the gospel, it becomes obvious that they are somewhat inadequate. As a result most evangelists expect that the new believer will need a lot more teaching in order to grow as a believer. Great emphasis is put on discipleship, in order to bring the new believer into a fuller understanding.

It's little wonder that western believers following the legal model of salvation, once they have invested something in the "life-insurance" aspect of salvation, are content to live their lives in comfort, as their view of salvation demands little else beyond confession of sin, and acceptance of a savior.

Legal Issues

It is interesting to notice that the legal view of salvation has legal problems. Many of the issues that Christians face today stem from their legal perspective of the gospel. These issues are then studied and debated in religious courts. These debates require the services of spiritual lawyers and judges to argue the different sides. We often call these spiritual lawyers, theologians, but in reality, many of them function as lawyers who carefully debate the legal problems that arise from the legal model of salvation.

1. Eternal Security

If a judge has pardoned you, are you pardoned for the past only or also for the present and future? This legal question, often classified as Arminianism versus Calvinism, is primarily a legal question that besets those who follow the legal model of salvation.

2. Sanctification

Is it possible to reach a place where you do not continue to break God's law, and where you become a 'law abiding citizen' in the Kingdom of God? This question requires that spiritual lawyers define sin and what it means to digress from God's law.

3. The Jewish law

The role of the Old Testament Mosaic Laws is also a problem for those who follow the legal model of salvation. Were the laws in the Old Testament God's laws? If they are God's laws, why don't we follow them today? Did Jesus fulfill all the laws, including the health laws about eating pork meat? Did God's law change?

This is just a sampling of the legal issues that spiritual lawyers spend countless hours and finances on. This action is not necessarily wrong, it is simply the natural outcome of our legal understanding of salvation.

My desire, however, is that rather than spending their time arguing the case for legal spiritual issues, theologians would wrestle with the best way to communicate the gospel to different people in different cultures.

My desire is that they would lift up their eyes and look at the fields that are white unto harvest, and put their theological training to work developing other approaches to salvation, that do not rely exclusively on legal thought and terminology. Shame-based cultures and fear-based cultures need other models for sharing salvation than the legal ones.

Conclusion

Just as an artist mixes colors of paints, cultures are made up of a mixture of elements. Very few cultures have ever been purely guilt-based, and many of the more or less guilt-based cultures in existence today are rapidly moving away from the influences of guilt. Many describe our present western culture as being post guilt.

In the next chapter we want to explore the second primary building block, that of fear. Once again there are few purely fear-based cultures in existence today, and as the world becomes more global, the purely fear-based cultures are giving way to a more mixed variety. Never the less, by looking briefly at fear-based cultures we can begin to recognize it when it is mixed in with guilt or shame.

CHAPTER FIVE

Fear-Based Cultures

As the missionaries drew near to the village, the sound of drums could be heard. Drawing closer, they could see people dancing and withering on the ground. A man approached the missionaries and explained that they could not go further. The village was doing a sacred rite to improve the economy and bring more trade to the area. They were escorted away and not given a chance to share their gospel presentation. Later the missionaries heard that a human sacrifice had been offered to the spirits that day.

In another situation missionaries arrived in a village when a rain-making ceremony was about to begin. They were invited to watch. A black bull was led to the edge of the village where it faced the direction from where the rain would come. The animal's throat was cut and it fell over on its left side, to the delight of all. This indicated that the sacrifice was acceptable. The men then cut up the meat and cooked it. As the meat was cooking, an old man began to shout out a prayer to the spirits for rain. Soon everyone joined in. After the meat was eaten, the shouting turned into dancing. The villagers danced all afternoon until the rain came. It rained so heavily that everyone had to run for shelter. Did the rituals bring the rain? To the natives it was obvious and there was no way that the missionaries could convince them otherwise.

As these two stories illustrate, there are many people in the world today whose lives revolve around their interaction with the spiritual world. They believe that gods and spirits exist in the universe and they must live in peace with these unseen powers, either by living quietly, or by appeasing these powers.

Much of the missionary effort during this last century has been directed at reaching people who live in areas of the world where elements of fear-based culture are strong. In the past, missionaries entering the jungles of Africa, South America, and other places such as Borneo were faced with people whose culture had strong elements of fear. While their beliefs varied from place to place and culture to culture the underlying principles were the same.

Based on their worldview, these cultures and peoples view the universe as a place filled with gods, demons, spirits, ghosts and ancestors. Man needs to live at peace with the powers around him, and often man lives in fear. This fear is based on a number of different things. First, man fears man. Tribal wars are endemic, with captives becoming slaves or, sometimes, a meal for cannibals. Whenever tribes encounter people from outside of their own group, they approached them with suspicion and fear.

Secondly, these people fear the supernatural. All around them events are taking place that can only be explained by the supernatural. Much like the ancient civilizations before Christ, they have developed spiritual explanations for how things work in this world. If crops fail, then specific gods or demons are responsible. If sickness comes, then other gods or demons are responsible. If a tribe fails in battle, it is because of the activity of a god or demon. Sickness is often viewed as a god reaping revenge. Everything in life, even romance, is somehow attributed to the activities of gods or demons.

The struggle that these people face is simply one of needing power. Using their voodoo, charms and other methods, they seek to gain control over other people and over the controlling powers of the universe. The paradigm that these people live in is one of fear versus power.

At the end of the 19th century, E.B. Tylor attempted to understand the difference in thinking between Europeans and other peoples living in Africa and South America. In his writings he coined the word 'animism' from the Latin word *anima* for 'soul.' He saw the *animistic* worldview as interpreting everything from a spiritual philosophy rather than a materialistic philosophy. Many sociologists of Tylor's era saw mankind moving from an ancient worldview based on the supernatural to a modern worldview based on science and reality.

Dave Burnett states in his book *Unearthly Powers,* that H. W. Turner later advocated the use of the term *primal religion,* meaning that "*these religions both anteceded the great historic religions and continue to reveal many of the basic or primary features of religion.*" Almost everywhere you find animists or primal religions you find people living under the influence of a fear-based culture.

Burnett goes on to state, "*Power can be understood in many ways: physical, political, economic, social, and religious. The secular worldview tends to regard all power as originating from within the material world.* . . . *In contrast, primal worldviews see such powers not only as being real within the empirical world but as having their primary origin outside the visible world.*"

In this way, those whose lives operate in the fear/power paradigm see themselves living in a physical world that co-exists and is influenced by unseen powers. These powers may be present in people or animals or even in inanimate objects like trees or hills. In some cultures, powers may be perceived in personal terms such as we would use for living beings. These powers are often regarded as having their own particular character, feeling and ability to relate to others, and often, even have a will of their own. Like people, they may be angered, placated or turned to in time of need.

Power is an important concept in fear-based cultures. In the Pacific Islands it is often called *mana,* while the Iroquois of North America call it *orenda,* which particularly refers to the mystic power derived from a chant. The Eskimos have the notion of *sila,* a force watching and controlling everything. The Chinese have the concept of *fung shui,* or the powers within the earth and sea. In folk Islam the term *baraka* (blessing or holiness) embraces many of these concepts.

In most fear/power cultures, the main way of dealing with a power is to establish rules to protect the unwary from harm and procedures to appease those powers that are offended. These rules and procedures are generally referred to as taboo. Taboos come in the form of things like special people, forbidden or unclean foods, sacred objects, and special names. Appeasements are usually made in the form of sacrifice or dedication to the invisible powers.

These powers can take various forms, such as: ghosts, ancestors who live around people, spirits in trees and rocks, and totems (clans associated with certain animals or inanimate objects.)

In order to deal with these powers, rituals are established which people believe will affect the powers around them. Rituals are performed on certain calendar dates, and at certain times in someone's life (rites of passage), or in a time of crisis.

In order to appease the powers of the universe, systems of appeasement are worked out. They vary from place to place. Some civilizations offer incense while some offer their children as sacrifices to gods. However it is done, a system of appeasement, based on fear is the norm for their worldview.

Wherever this system of appeasement comes into being, religious persons come to the forefront to control these systems. In some cases they are known as priests. In other cases they are known as witch doctors, or shamans. Whatever their title, their role is the same. They are the ones who understand the needs of the gods or demons, and they are the ones through whom the demons or gods communicate.

In every fear-based culture, the pattern is much the same. The witch doctor, priest or shaman controls people through the use of fear. They are very effective in their roles, and as a result, whole cultures and people groups are held in their iron grip.

As missionaries have entered these areas, they have found themselves confronted with a power struggle. Shamans, priests, and witch doctors hold considerable spiritual power. It is real power, backed by the satanic world. Satan and his hosts are determined to keep fear-based cultures in their grip. In almost every case, a power struggle develops when missionaries confront fear-based cultures.

Over time, Christian missionaries have learned to share the gospel in such a way that it makes sense to those living in fear. Missionaries have shared the stories in the Bible and have brought people to the conclusion that the power that is available through Christ is greater than the powers of darkness. Missionaries have shared from God's Word, demonstrated God's power, and have lived out their Christian lives for all to see. As they have boldly preached, and confronted the powers of the enemy, people in these cultures have begun turning from darkness to light.

As a result, today in Africa, South America, and East Asia there are large numbers of people who have come to Christ from a fear-based cultural background.

Conclusion

From the Garden of Eden we see that the influence of sin brought more than guilt upon mankind. It also brought fear. This fear is very real to many people in the world today. Some cultures can be described as being almost totally fear-based. Many other cultures mix aspects of fear-based worldview with the other building blocks: guilt and shame. Some elements of fear-based culture are even present in today's western world where people consult physics, and dabble in the occult. Even closer to home are some of our fears of certain numbers and events, like breaking a mirror or allowing a black cat to cross our paths. To some people these are very serious events, while others laugh them off. While it may not be important to some, fear and power are fundamental to many people's worldview. As Christians, it is out duty to share the love and grace available through Christ in such a way that people in a fear based culture can clearly understand.

CHAPTER SIX

Shame-Based Cultures

The guilt/innocence perspective in which we live dictates much of our thinking in the west. However, not everyone in the world operates within this paradigm. As I mentioned earlier, while living in the Middle East I noticed that when the lifeguard blew his whistle, the westerners all stopped to see who was guilty, but the Arabs kept right on swimming.

As I observed this and other phenomena, I began to realize that Arabs and Arab society were operating in another whole dimension. Guilt did not have the same power and influence as it did in the west. While they were aware of guilt, it didn't have the same strong connotations for them as it had for me.

If a policeman pulled me over, I immediately felt guilty, thinking that perhaps I had done something wrong. But when my Arab friends were pulled over, they didn't display any sign of guilt. They talked boldly to the policeman, and even argued loudly with him over the issues at hand.

It was only after many years of living in a Muslim culture that it started to dawn on me that the Arabs around me were not operating on a level of guilt versus innocence. Nor were they operating in a fear versus power paradigm. I had heard much about this from missionaries living in Africa but it didn't seem to apply to the Arabs of the Levant. Rather, I discovered that Arabs were living in a worldview where the paradigm was shame versus honor.

Once I clued in to this, I began to explore this concept and tried to verify it on all social levels. I was amazed to discover what

I found. When a young Christian lady, who was very active in the church, was asked why she was so dedicated, she said that she feared that God would shame her in front of people; so she worked hard in the church. I was appalled at first, until I recognized this same motivating factor at work in many situations.

When I would visit my friends, I would try to act correctly and they would try to act honorably, not shamefully. I was busy trying to learn the rights and wrongs of their culture and explain them to new people arriving from the west. But somehow my framework of right versus wrong didn't fit what was actually happening. The secret wasn't to act rightly or wrongly in their culture. It wasn't that there was a right way and a wrong way of doing things. The underlying principle was that there was an honorable and dishonorable way of doing things.

Every part of the Muslim culture I lived in was based on honor and shame. When I visited my friends I could honor them in the way I acted. They could honor me, in the way they acted. Three cups of coffee bestowed honor on me. The first, called 'salam' (peace) was followed by 'sadaqa' (friendship), and the third cup of coffee was called 'issayf' (the sword). The meaning was clear in their culture. When I arrived I was offered a cup of coffee that represented peace between us. As we drank and talked, the cup of friendship was offered. The last cup, the sword, illustrated their willingness to protect me and stand by me. It didn't matter if I was right or wrong, they were bound by their honor to protect me.

Everything in the Middle Eastern cultures I moved in pointed to honor or shame. What chair I chose to sit in, who entered the door first, the way I expressed myself in Arabic, the very way I walked and held myself, all communicated to others around me my place in the world. The cultures of the Middle East are filled with thousands of tiny nuances that communicate either shame or honor.

Shame is a popular topic today. In our western society, shame is closely identified with a lack of self-esteem. Shame often stems from some form of abuse where children fail to learn trust. This is quite different from the shame societies of the east where shame and fear of shame are used as controlling forces in people's lives.

As parents, we teach our children to act rightly. If they don't, we teach them that feelings of guilt are the proper response. In a shame-based culture, children are taught to act honorably, and if they don't, feelings of shame are the proper response. But it goes farther than just feelings. Shame and honor are positions in society, just as being right (and justified) is a position in our western culture.

In the west, young people are free to act as spontaneously as they want, as long as they are within the framework of right and wrong. They can be loud, boisterous and happy, as long as they don't break things, or abuse others. Our rule in the west is "As long as I don't hurt someone else or their property, I'm generally ok."

Young people in a Muslim setting are different. Wherever they go, they represent their families and tribes. Young people are not free to act as they want. They must always act honorably, so that the honor of their family and tribe is upheld.

If they act shamefully, then the family or tribe will react against them. Shameful deeds are covered up. If they can't be covered up, they are revenged. It is the unwritten rule of the desert. The whole concept of shameful deeds can be traced back to the early Bedouin code of practice, which existed even before Islam arrived. This code, still much in existence today, affects not only the way individuals act, but also the actions of entire nations.

As I have visited with missionaries and nationals from other eastern countries, I have continued to explore the concept of honor and shame among these other countries. It has helped me understand and communicate with people from Afghanistan, Pakistan, India, China, Japan and Korea.

In fact, I have discovered that the concept of shame and honor makes a great discussion topic. I have often asked people from shame-based cultures what are honorable or shameful acts or actions in their cultures. The discussion that follows is often highly stimulating, and usually reflects or contrasts similar attitudes right across the shame-based countries of the world.

As an example, when visiting the Gateway Center for Cross-cultural Communication in Langley, British Columbia on Canada's western coast, I participated in a discussion about Korean students. A Korean missiologist was visiting and we started to discuss the Korean students that were studying in the Gateway school. The Gateway staff had noticed that all of the Korean men were very quiet while their wives were the ones who usually talked.

The Korean missiologist then explained to us that in Korea men were taught to be quiet. I then entered the discussion and brought up the topic of acting honorably. The Korean man brightened considerably, and began to explain how Korean men are taught to act honorably. One of the signs of honor is to hold off speaking until you have something wise to say.

He then went on to share how one well known Korean pastor only spoke from the pulpit. In his church ministry he basically never spoke to anyone else. A Korean once joked that perhaps this pastor never even spoke to his wife and kids. We laughed and then went on to discuss how Korean women were free to speak and thus they were the ones who spoke out, not their husbands. As a result, Korean women are the ones who usually learn languages better.

A few weeks later I spoke to a medical doctor from Iraq and told her what I had learned from the Koreans. She immediately responded that in the older Iraqi culture this was true as well, especially among the older men. Honor is demonstrated by silence, and speaking only wise and careful things. Often the speech of wise people is full of proverbs and parables. The more proverbs a person knows, the wiser he appears in the eyes of others.

In some cases however, there are distinct differences between cultures. As I mentioned earlier, if someone is badly shamed in an

Arab culture and the shame cannot be hidden, then it is revenged, and the person responsible for the shaming is killed. In many eastern cultures, if a shame cannot be hidden, the way out is suicide. Even here, however, there are many similarities, as I have known of a number of students in Jordan committing suicide because of their poor school marks, just as happens in Japan.

In order for shame-based cultures to work, shame and honor are usually attached to something greater than the individual. Honor is almost always placed on a group. This can be the immediate family, the extended tribe, or in some cases, as large as an entire nation; as was demonstrated in Japan just previous to World War Two.

In most Middle Eastern cultures, honor is wrapped up with one's tribe. Everyone grows up within a tribal concept. If someone is from the Beni Hassan tribe, he thinks and acts, and dresses as a Beni Hassan. His actions reflect on the honor the Beni Hassan tribe. If he acts honorably, the Beni Hassan tribe is honored. If he acts shamefully, the whole tribe is shamed. If the act is vile enough, the Beni Hassan tribe will react, and execute the offender, even though he is a member of their own tribe, and perhaps even their immediate family. Thus the honor of the tribe is restored.

Many years ago an Arab soldier's gun accidentally discharged and killed his friend and companion in the army. After serving seven years, he was released on condition that he leave Jordan. He lived for nearly twenty years in the United States, but decided to return one day to see his family. When it was learned that he had returned, several young people, some of whom had not been born at the time of the killing, surrounded the house where he was and riddled his body with bullets. Their honor was restored, and shame removed.

If someone shames another tribe, tribal warfare could result, and often only the skilful intervention of a third party ends the strife. Arab lore is full of stories of how wise and skillful men have intervened in difficult situations. In fact, many national rulers gain their fame and reputation from their skills at ending tribal strife.

In the Middle East two methods are recognized. First, a skillful ruler, through diplomatic efforts and displays of great wisdom, can end disputes. Solomon's dealings with the two mothers who claimed the same baby displayed the kind of wisdom that Arabs appreciate and desire in their rulers. The second kind of ruler crushes all of the tribes and by force makes them submit to himself. Peace may then rule, but once the controlling power is removed, old animosities return. This is well illustrated in the Balkans conflict where the domination of communism brought about a measure of peace. Once freedom returned however, old conflicts and animosities flared again.

The storytellers who frequent the coffeehouses of the Middle East excel in telling stories of both kinds of rulers and heroes, especially heroes who can effectively deal with shame and restore honor. This is very different from the entertainment styles of the west, where the hero determines who is guilty, and punishes him, and right and goodness reign again. This is because in our worldview, we try to hang onto the concept that in the midst of a crooked and perverse world, right still reigns and has the upper hand. Those from a shame-based culture, on the other hand, cling to the idea of maintaining honor, in the midst of a shameful and alienated world.

For many western people it is very hard if not impossible to try and comprehend a culture that is based on shame, not right versus wrong. In *Tools for Muslim Evangelism* I gave a number of examples of how this affects the Muslim cultures of the Middle East. I won't repeat that material here, but I would like to add to it the illustration of telling the truth.

In our culture, telling the truth is right and telling lies is wrong. In the Middle East, people don't think of lies as being right or wrong. The question is, "Is what is being said, honorable." If a lie protects the honor of a tribe or nation, then it is fine. If a lie is told for purely selfish reasons, then it is shameful.

Thus, in the west we debate ethics, by trying to determine if things are right or wrong. In the east, they debate ethics, by trying to determine if things are honorable or not.

Shame in Our Culture

In the past, shame has played a role in our culture. One has only to read Tolstoy's *Anna Karenina*, or any of Shakespeare's works to see the role that shame used to play. Shakespeare uses the word shame nine times as often as he does guilt. In our evangelical world, old Christian songs mention Christ's death on the cross for our 'sin and shame' while most songs from the last century tend to mention our 'sin and guilt.'

Why is this? I suspect that the popularity of Freud's teachings is one reason. Sociologists generally credit Freudian psychology for the removal of guilt from our culture. Since his teachings have become popular in our universities, the concept of guilt has become unpopular and guilt has been assigned to others, such as our parents. Other factors, like the lack of responsibility within modern politics have influence young people today. Nixon and Watergate, and Clinton and Lewinsky have illustrated to people today that 'right versus wrong' is not the only way to think.

During the period of 1960 to 2000 western civilization has begun a slow but steady shift towards the shame/honor paradigm. Today young people are very reluctant to label anything as right or wrong. Instead, things are assigned the label as "cool" or "not cool." In the eyes of many high school students, being cool is equivalent to being honorable. Being not cool is the equivalent of shame. I believe that this slow shift in worldview is responsible for many of the differences between boosters, boomers, busters and Generation X'rs.

Shaming in History

Roman culture started out in the fear/power paradigm. Events of nature and history were interpreted within this paradigm. The worship of a pantheon of gods carried on during their whole civilization until Christianity became the state religion. When the Romans adopted the Greek pattern of placing the law above the emperor, they began to interpret events in their society on the guilt/innocence paradigm. This soon came to the forefront of their civilization, and fear/power was pushed to the back.

When the Romans conquered shame-based civilizations the people they conquered had a profound impact on their own culture. Shame was always present in Roman culture, but it slowly came more and more to the forefront and eventually into Mediterranean culture today.

In republican Rome, criminals had the doors to their houses burned as a public sign that a criminal was living there. Those who had been wronged could follow the criminal around, chanting and accusing him in public places.

The concept of public shaming carried on into the Middle Ages, and even into Victorian England where criminals were put into stocks. These stocks were located in public places, so that the criminal would be known and shamed before all. Pillories were rife until the Victorian age, when those who were pilloried had to endure the shame of publicly having rotten vegetables thrown at them. Branding criminals was practiced in England until the eighteenth century. Brands were often placed on the hands or face, so that the criminals would be publicly shamed wherever they went.

The major difference between east and west, however, is not the presence of the shame concept, but rather, the structure of society around either the group mentality or individualism. Eastern shame became much more powerful than western shaming activities, simply because in the east the shame rests on the person's group rather than the individual. Since eastern society functions in a group setting, the whole group suffers rather than just the individual.

If the crime is bad enough, the group may oust or, for a severe offense, kill the offender.

In 1999 at least twenty-five women were killed to maintain the honor of their families in the country of Jordan. Hundreds of others were killed in countries like Egypt, Sudan, Syria and Iran. In many countries where shame-based culture is predominant, the names of criminals and those being ousted from their families for shameful activities are publicly printed in the newspapers. In western countries we tend to isolate criminals from their surroundings, and then determine if they are guilty. Criminals are then locked away out of sight, rather than publicly shamed in stocks in the public square.

It's interesting to notice that in the Crow Indian culture in North America, mocking of some one else's inappropriate behavior effects shaming. This is sometimes called *"buying-of-the-ways."* If you imitate someone else's inappropriate behavior, you are buying his ways. In some cases a person actually offers money to buy someone else's inappropriate behavior. This is the ultimate shame.

In many shame-based cultures, rather than encourage others, people criticize and question others. This is seen as positive, as it keeps them from becoming too proud.

Ken Guenther, in his paper *Pain in a Shame Culture, Help for the Filipino Pastor,* (a 1997 term paper for Dr. James Houston, Regent College) states: *"Because the pastor may be perceived as distant, his motives may be questioned, which is the most painful form of shame for the Filipino. Once the leader is seen to be going too far in his exercise of authority or to be too ambitious or proud, he is put down through the moral mechanism of shaming. The widely recognized "crab mentality" of Filipino culture is an illustration of this mechanism . . . . In a shame culture, however, mere success is not sufficient (it is not enough, for example, to know in your own mind that you are the best); public acknowledgment of one's superiority is essential."*

In the same way, Arabs are often quick to criticize leaders and pastors if they perceive that they are too ambitious or proud. They are sometimes publicly questioned or shamed, and often they leave the ministry. Even new language students discover that their neighbors are quick to point out that someone else speaks better than they do, or they are asked why they speak so poorly after being there for "a whole four months!" The criticism is often meant to keep them from being proud of how well they have done. Arabs understand that the criticism may be a compliment, but the poor westerner is often crushed.

Conclusion

While all cultures have certain elements of shame, there are cultures that are primarily built on the worldview of shame versus honor. Just as guilt, fear and shame came upon mankind in the Garden of Eden, guilt, shame and fear exist in all cultures today. What makes a shame-based culture unique is that its people relate almost everything to the shame-honor paradigm, rather than to the guilt-righteousness or the fear-power paradigm.

The question that we as Christians must ask then, is: What does the Bible say about all of this? Does the Bible have a clear message of God's grace that can be expressed with shame and honor terminology rather than with legal terminology? I strongly believe it does, and this is what we will look into in the next chapter.

CHAPTER SEVEN

Honor and Shame in the Bible

Mohammed was a Jordanian friend of mine. He worked for the post office, and the secret police. His job was to read mail that came into the country where I was working. After a while, he discovered that the mail that came to my post box was rather interesting and he put into motion a plan to meet the owner of the post box. It wasn't long before he offered to relieve the guard at the post office door, and that evening he saw me take mail from my post box. The next day I returned, and Mohammed made his move. We met and a friendship developed. Soon Mohammed had a copy of the Bible to read.

One night, Mohammed arrived at my house, obviously agitated. After the traditional cup of tea, Mohammed closed the windows to my living room, and sat close beside me, speaking almost in a whisper. His reading of the Bible had progressed smoothly until he had arrived at I Samuel 2:8. It was Hannah's song of praise to God for giving her baby Samuel. When Mohammed arrived at verse 8, he found something that he couldn't cope with. Hannah said " *He (God) raises the poor from the dust and lifts up the needy* (beggars in the Arabic Bible) *from the ash heap; he seats them with princes and has them inherit a throne of honor.*"

Mohammed threw the Bible down on the coffee table. "No," he said emphatically. "This cannot be true. A beggar is a beggar, a prince is a prince. This is garbage."

As I stared at Mohammed's face, I suddenly saw a truth I had never seen before. This wasn't garbage; this was the gospel. I Samuel

2:8 describes the gospel in terms of God taking us from the shame of sin, and raising us to being joint heirs with Christ. I was only 22 years of age at the time, and just beginning my ministry in the Middle East, but God used this incident to start me down the path of understanding His plan for mankind in the area of shame and honor.

Our western culture has lost most of our understanding of shame and honor but the Bible is filled with it. The Bible begins with man's fall into shame and ends with His being anointed with glory and honor at God's right hand.

All through the Bible, references are made to shame and honor in various forms. The Bible tells us to honor God, our parents, elders, Christian leaders, and government leaders. It even talks about certain things being more honorable than others. In all, there are more than 190 references to honor in the Bible, while the various forms of the word 'guilt' are mentioned only forty times, and only seven of these are in the New Testament.

The Bible also addresses shame, mentioning it over one hundred times. But simply counting the word 'shame' is not enough. There are many underlying principles in the Bible that deal with shame and honor, and demonstrate how God moves us from a position of shame to that of honor. The whole point of mentioning these numbers is simply to illustrate that shame and honor hold a place in the Bible along side of teachings about guilt and righteousness.

The main reason God allowed His people to fall into slavery in Egypt was to demonstrate to all the shame-based nations and cultures in the Middle East the power of Jehovah God in raising his people from a position of shame in Egypt to one of honor among the nations. Leviticus 26:13 states, *"I am the Lord your God, who brought you out of Egypt so that you would no longer be slaves to the Egyptians; I broke the bars of your yoke and enabled you to walk with heads held high."*

This is the overall message of the Bible. It is not just the story of God redeeming His people (a legal thought), but it is also the story of God raising mankind from a position of shame, to the ultimate position of joint-heir with Christ.

In the following pages, I have outlined a series of topics from the Scriptures that teach us how God is moving us from a position of shame to that of honor. The position of shame is described in the Bible in a series of ways: defiled, naked, sick, poor, accursed, ignorant and so on. Each of these topics is a powerful illustration of God's desire and power to move us from shame to honor. Only one of these topics includes legal terms or concepts. All the others use personal and community concepts that are applicable in most shame-based cultures.

Almost everyone in a shame-based culture knows of someone who is acting more honorable that he or she really is. People laugh at them behind their backs. At one time, I was told by friends that my landlord wasn't as big a man as he made out to be. He drove a Mercedes car, dressed in fine suit coats, and had four boys. He walked the streets very piously and in an honorable fashion, but everyone knew he was just a little man, holding a minor government position and no special position in his tribe. He was not the big man he made himself out to be.

And so it is, that we come to the message of *grace* in the Bible. God is the one who can elevate people from a position of shame to that of honor. No one can elevate himself. This is the unwritten rule of the east. Everyone knows their place, and must stay in it. The message of the Gospel is that God has the power and the desire to elevate man from his lowly position to a place of great honor. *"See, I lay a stone in Zion, a chosen and precious cornerstone, and the one who trust in Him will never be put to shame."* I Peter 2:6.

Each of the topics mentioned below illustrates this point, and has numerous Biblical references that can be used. These topics make great conversation starters, Bible study notes, or even sermon outlines. They are the kind of thing that those ministering to people from shame-based cultures must be well versed in.

God moves us from being defiled to being cleansed

Many eastern religions concentrate on ritual washings. Before a man can enter a mosque to pray, he must remove his shoes and wash. His shoes are symbols of the dirt that contaminates his life by living and walking in a defiled world. He removes his shoes and washes according to the age-old traditions and teachings of Islam. Then he can approach God in prayer, without shame.

In Muslim culture, shame and honor are attached to places and locations as well as to actions. Some places are more honorable than others. Some are more shameful. A man can pray at home or in the market, but it is better to pray at the local mosque as the mosque has greater honor. Holy sites have even greater honor, and the Kaba in Mecca is the most honorable of all.

Before picking up the Qur'an to read, a Muslim must wash. Living in an evil world defiles his hands. After washing, he has removed the contamination that disqualified him from reading and hearing from God. Now he is deemed worthy.

After having relations with his wife, a Muslim man must bath in order to be clean. If he does not, the very ground he walks on will become defiled. Once again, after ritual washing, he can approach God, but not before purification has occurred.

In most shame-based cultures the Christian can make an immediate connection between defilement and cleansing and the grace of God as revealed in the Bible. The Old Testament is full of this imagery:

In Exodus 30 we see that Aaron and his sons were to wash their hands and feet whenever they entered the tent of meeting or approached the altar; otherwise they would die. Their actions portrayed a picture of what was to come in Christ, who provided cleansing through the washing of the blood.

Leviticus 13 & 14 are about the cleansing of a leper. Remember that lepers were in a tremendous position of shame, even to the point of being isolated and having to go around crying out "unclean, unclean." Yet, in Leviticus 14, God provides a way of cleansing, at the instigation of the priest, not the leper. It is possible to make many comparisons between the cleansing of the leper and salvation.

Also, in the Gospels, Jesus continually turned to the lepers to heal them, demonstrating God's desire to reach out to those in a place of shame, and restore them.

In the Old Testament, blemished or defective animals were not permitted for sacrificial use. Items used for worship had to be anointed or consecrated. Unclean animals could not be used. Jesus, however, in Mark 7:18-23 challenged the Pharisees in their use and understanding of cleansing and dietary laws, affirming that man himself is unclean.

The issue of cleanness centers on man's basic condition. In the west, we often list man's sinful condition with a variety of legal words. How many of us include in that list that man is in a position of defilement? The law was put in place, not only to point out man's guilt and need of a savior, but to also point out man's defilement and need for a cleanser. Just as the Old Testament offerings drew attention to man's need for a sacrifice for sin, the acts of cleansing pointed out man's need for washing and purification from defilement.

Just as Christ's work on the cross once and for all removed our sin, it also, once for all, removed our defilement. *"The blood of goats and bulls and the ashes of a heifer sprinkled on those who were ceremonially unclean sanctify them so they were outwardly clean. How much more, then, will the blood of Christ, who through the eternal Spirit offered himself unblemished to God, cleanse our consciences from acts that lead to death, so that we may serve the living God."* Hebrews 9:13,14

Cleansing is fundamental to understanding grace. Mankind is unclean. It is not just that man is totally depraved, mankind is totally defiled.

If you use this paradigm, then New Testament stories about the cleansing of the lepers (Luke 5:12-14) and the Gentile woman who was defiled in the eyes of the Jews (Matthew 15:21-28) and the Jewish woman who bled for 12 years and was thus unclean for 12 years, and unable to enter the temple (Mark 5:25-35) will become part of your teaching. These are the kind of verses that speak loud and clear to those living in shame-based cultures, and in need of a Cleanser, a Savior and a Redeemer.

From Naked to Clothed

In reinforcing our message of God's provision for shame, the illustration can be used of how God takes us naked, and clothes us.

In the Garden of Eden, man's shame stemmed in part from man's nakedness. The New Testament tells us that our proper clothing is eternal, and that we groan and long to be clothed with it (II Corinthians 5:1-2). When Adam and Eve sinned, they lost their eternal life, and immediately felt naked and exposed. Until we reach heaven and are clothed with our eternal clothing, we will be in a position of nakedness and shame. II Corinthians 5 is a very useful chapter in explaining the Gospel to those who are from a shame-based culture. Many of Paul's illustrations and the whole basis of his teaching in this chapter demonstrates to the reader how God will someday clothe us with immortality.

However you want to state it theologically, nakedness and shame go together, and can be a useful tool to use when sharing from the scriptures. The story of our nakedness and shame must start in Genesis 3. Job tells us in Job 1:21 that we were born naked, and the picture can be drawn of our shame and nakedness right from birth.

The Old Testament law contains many references to nakedness, and gives many rules concerning whom one could marry. From the Old Testament law it is obvious that there can be many shameful relationships between people. Leviticus 18 is full of references to shameful relationships that were not to be among God's redeemed people. The word used all through Leviticus 18 is 'nakedness.'

Isaiah says, *"I delight greatly in the Lord; my soul rejoices in my God. For he has clothed me with garments of salvation and arrayed me in a rob of righteousness, as a bridegroom adorns his head like a priest, and as a bride adorns herself with her jewels."*

In the New Testament, Jesus told the story of the prodigal son, who returned home full of shame for what he had done. When his father welcomed him home, the first thing his father commanded was that a robe be brought for his son (Luke 15:22). In the same way, the first thing God does for his returning children is to raise them from a position of shame to a place of honor, by covering us with the robe of righteousness.

The ultimate picture of God bearing our shame is found in Christ who was stripped of His clothing when He was hung on the cross. Roman prisoners were often hung naked on a cross, exposed for the scoffers to see and ridicule. Consequently, even in this, Christ bore, not only our sin on the cross, but also our shame. Once for all, Christ died on the cross, bearing our shame, so that we might be freed from shame as well as guilt.

There are many more references to nakedness and clothing, but in the final pages of the Bible, we are told of how the believers will be clothed in heaven. At the Marriage Supper of the Lamb, we will come forth in our wedding garments, made from our own righteous acts. Right from Genesis to Revelation we see the unfolding plan of man, starting out naked and ashamed, but he is clothed through God's grace provided by Christ on the cross.

From Expelled (from Eden and God) to Visited by God

In shame-based cultures, everyone knows how important it is to belong to a family or tribe. This is part of the 'group' mindset. Your group provides you with what you need in life. Everything from fellowship, money, opportunity, education, a spouse, and security are obtained through the group. A man without a group is in an impossible situation.

A Jordanian television series several years back dealt with the issues that arose when a man found himself in the shameful position of no longer having a family. The very act of being thrown out of your family is considered the ultimate shame. It is worsened in many countries when the expulsion story is announced in the newspaper so everyone knows that the person has been shamed.

And so, man was shamed when he was expelled from the Garden of Eden. The very act of expulsion added to man's shame. He was cast out of his home, and away from the presence of his father.

All through history man has lived separated from God. Even the Muslim can tell you that you cannot go into the presence of God, because God is honorable, and you are in a position of shame.

The whole message of the Gospel revolves around the restoration of the relationship between man and God. Man is not in a position to elevate himself. Only God can restore the one who is ousted. Secondly, God used a mediator. Mediators must be able to speak on equal terms with both God and man, and so Jesus became human, in order to mediate between us. And it is only through the person of Jesus that a way is made so that our relationship with God can be restored. Through Jesus man moves from being expelled to being accepted. We now have access to God's throne room. We are now called sons of God, and God even elevates us to the position of being a joint-heir with Jesus.

A friend of mine once preached a sermon on John 17, where Jesus prays to the Father, and says these amazing words: *"I have given them the glory you have given me, that they may be one as we are one: I in them and you in me. May they be brought to complete unity to let the world now that you send me and have loved them even as you have loved me."* He went on to explain that Jesus has bestowed on every believer the glory and honor that God the Father bestowed on his son Jesus. Our position now is that of a joint-heir. Once we are in heaven we will fully enter into our inheritance.

The pastor and the congregation had many questions afterwards. They couldn't believe that this type of honor was possible.

Somehow the Arab pastor's western theological education had never introduced him to the concept of God's honoring of the saints.

These are powerful concepts for those from a shame-based culture. People can accept that God honored Jesus, because He was the Son of God and sinless and thus deserved honor. But the Bible says that Jesus has also glorified us and has given us the same honor. This honor is ultimately demonstrated in heaven where we are rewarded and honored, even to the place of being joint-heirs with Christ. The heir always has the ultimate honor in any tribe and we are included in this honor.

From Weakness to Strength

The Bible makes numerous references to weakness. Man is in a weak condition, and often unable to help himself. He easily succumbs to sin and falls quickly into temptation. Many people want to be stronger, but lack the will power.

One day, while traveling in a taxi, the driver offered me a cigarette. When I refused, he commented that I must be very strong to resist the pressure. This provided a wonderful opportunity to share about the one who makes weak people strong.

Isaiah tells us, *"He gives strength to the weary, and increases the power of the weak. Even youths grow tired and weary, and young men stumble and fall; but those who hope in the Lord will renew their strength. They will soar on wings like eagles; they will run and not grow weary, they will walk and not be faint."* Isaiah 40:29-31

Jesus, in his earthly ministry, displayed a kind of strength that is passed on to the believers. Strength to stand in the day of trial. Strength to endure. Strength to withstand the enemy, in Jesus' name.

Grace and strength are tied together in 2 Corinthians 12:9 when Paul *says "But he (God) said to me, My grace is sufficient for you, for my power is made perfect in weakness. Therefore I will boast all the more gladly about my weaknesses, so that Christ's power may rest on me."*

Peter adds in I Peter 5:10 *"And the God of all grace who called you to his eternal glory in Christ, after you have suffered a little while, will himself restore you and make you strong, firm and steadfast."*

The message of God's grace includes the concept that God wants to move us from a place of weakness to a place of strength; not our own strength, but Christ in us, the hope of glory, who is our strength.

From sickness to being healed

Why did Jesus spend so much time healing the sick? Part of the answer lies in the picture we have in the Bible of God moving man from a place of sickness to a place of freedom from sickness.

Part of the curse in Genesis is man's physical death. As soon as he is born, man begins the slow process of dying; and part of the dying process is sickness.

In Exodus 23:25, God told the children of Israel that if they obeyed his commands He would bless them and take sickness away from their land. However, in Deuteronomy 28:58-61 God warns them that if they do not obey His commands then God will bring sickness upon them as a punishment.

Sickness is one of the results of man's shameful and sinful position. It is part of the judgement of God on the entire human race. But through the person of Jesus, God demonstrates His power over sickness. In the book of Revelation, God tells us that in heaven there will be no more sickness and pain, (21:4) for they are part of the former things. Isaiah 53:5 says of the Messiah: *"by his wounds we are healed."*

God's ultimate plan of salvation can be demonstrated through God's plan to bring us from a place of sickness to a place of being healed, not only physically, but emotionally and spiritually as well. That is why we read that in heaven there will be no more sickness and no more tears.

As you can see from the examples above, there are many ways of explaining the gospel to people, without using legal terminology. Instead of expounding on more topics, I will simply list a number of other topics that I have heard ministers from a shame-based culture use to explain the gospel message to their own people.

- From dying to being raised
- From a place that is far from God to being indwelt by God's Spirit
- From imprisoned in the flesh to being gifted in the Spirit
- From spiritually poor to having riches in God
- From failure and falling short to being made complete in Christ
- From being illegitimate children to being a child of God
- From ignorant to being taught of God
- From blind to seeing
- From darkness to being enlightened by God
- From stumbling to being strengthened & encouraged
- From accused to being exonerated/represented
- From cursed to being blessed
- From tiredness to being renewed
  And finally . . . .
- From guilty to being redeemed

Yes, we should not forget this one. Legal concepts should be explained using the legal terminology of the culture. If a redemption analogy is used in the culture, as it is in most Islamic cultures, then it can be useful to help demonstrate how God provides an answer to sin through the substitutionary death of Jesus on the Cross.

Once the person has understood how God is moving us from a position of shame to a position of honor, he can then move on to understanding God's plan to move us from being guilty to a place of receiving redemption.

Conclusion

When working with people who do not have a clear understanding of what guilt is, we should start explaining the gospel by showing from the scriptures how God wants to lift us from a position of shame to that of honor. This usually takes some time, and a lot of explaining. The Bible is talking of spiritual riches, not physical. The Bible is talking of God honoring us, not of us walking around with our noses in the air. In fact, Jesus makes it plain in the Sermon on the Mount, that God honors the humble, not the proud. If God honors the proud, they only get more proud. But when the humbled are honored, they simply grow more humble and turn the honor onto the one honoring them.

When you feel that your audience has sufficiently accepted the fact that God wants to move them from shame to honor, you can begin to explain to them what guilt is all about.

God did this for the children of Israel in the book of Leviticus. Starting in Leviticus 1, God begins to define what guilt is, and how presenting a 'guilt offering' can make the person clean again. Many of us take the instructions in Leviticus for granted, but for those coming out of the Egyptian Fear/Power worldview, and living in the Semitic Shame/Honor worldview, clear instructions were needed to define guilt.

As an aside, I have discovered that, when explaining God's judgement to people from a shame-based culture, it is important to emphasize that God will not publicly shame the believer when He judges us in heaven. There is a vast difference between the Great White Throne Judgement and the Judgement Seat of Christ, (often simply called the 'seat of Christ.')

At the Great White Throne Judgement (Revelation 20:11-15), all the lost (dead) of the world are gathered, and all are judged, in front of everyone else, and all pass on to the lake of fire. At the Judgement Seat of Christ, however, believers are judged individually and in private. This happens as soon as we die. We are absent from the body and immediately present with the Lord. This is not a judgement to determine guilt and punishment, but rather an assessment to determine rewards. It is not something to be dreaded, and it is not a place where we will be publicly shamed. In fact, I Corinthians 3:8 tells us that every man shall receive a reward according to his own labor.

From the Scriptures we can see that God is not in the business of shaming his followers. Rather, he is in the business of lifting us up from shame. Many well meaning Bible teachers from a guilt-based worldview have inadvertently put great fear into believers from shame-based worldviews, by teaching about God's judgment, without mentioning that God will honor His children, and publicly condemn and shame those who have rejected him. Romans 8:1 tells us that there is now no condemnation to those who are in Christ Jesus. Condemnation is reserved for those who will stand before the Great White Throne Judgement. Through the cross of Christ, God has removed our guilt, our shame and our fear.

In the following chapter, I would like to examine what happens when worldviews clash. Then I would like to look at Islam in the Middle East as a case study of how a shame-based culture works. In Chapter eleven I would then like to draw this all to a conclusion by examining what a clear presentation of the gospel should contain, if it is to address all three aspects of fear, shame and guilt.

CHAPTER EIGHT

Clash of World Views

As I mentioned earlier, there are three basic planes on which worldview, function. On each of these planes, there is a basic tension between two extremes. The three planes are:

Guilt <——> Innocence

Shame <——> Honor

Fear <——> Power

It is possible to find all three dynamics in most cultures, but usually one or two are more dominant. Some cultures, however, operate almost entirely within one major paradigm. Secondly, cultures and worldviews are constantly shifting. The shift may be slow or fast depending on the events of history.

As an example, at the founding of the Roman Empire, the citizens of Rome operated almost entirely in a fear/power worldview, worshiping a pantheon of gods. As their civilization developed, they introduced the idea of law being higher than the emperor. In this one step they began to introduce the concept of guilt and innocence. As their civilization developed they moved almost completely away from the fear/power worldview. However, as their empire expanded they slowly introduced into it shades of the shame/honor worldview. One only has to watch the Godfather movies to see how guilt/innocence and shame/honor are the two planes that many Italians moved in during that era. Today, however, southern European culture has almost entirely lost its guilt/innocence perspective on life. Almost anything is acceptable today.

The Freudian question of *why you have so much guilt?* is not the question society is asking today. Today people are asking, *"Who am I?"* People are seeking to discover who they are, and want to find an identity. Several things consume us:

. Who am I and how can I express myself?
. How can I enjoy myself?
. Am I fully exercising my rights?
. What are my options in life and am I able to choose?

Dr. James Houston of Regent College in Vancouver, Canada, thinks that in our post modern North American culture, guilt is being replaced by shame. As I mentioned earlier, the concept of something being 'cool' or 'not cool' seems to have many similarities to shame and honor-based thinking.

We must be careful here, not to try and make cultures and worldviews fit into one of the three categories: guilt, shame or fear. All cultures are made up of a mixture of all three, and individual families and even individuals in the west identify with different worldviews.

As an example, in one family you may have an individual who is an evangelical Christian with strong traditional roots. This person may relate much of life to guilt/innocence thinking. A teenager in the same family may not quite see everything as so black and white and may be reluctant to accept things as being right or wrong. Rather, he or she wants to be seen as cool and desires to act and dress as cool. To be anything less would be humiliating. At the same time, a third member of the family may be into the occult, psychics and horoscopes. He or she may see life as being influenced by the stars and occultic powers. Thus, in one family, you may have people who seem to be holding three completely different worldviews.

When digging deeper, however, you may find that these people do not hold strictly to one or the other of these mega-trends, but that they have adopted some of each of them into their lives.

This can be illustrated by looking at North American native cultures. Most of these cultures are made up of a mixture of shame/honor and fear/power worldviews. One North American native I spoke to recently seemed to be torn between seeking revenge for someone who had shamed him, and wanting to pray for him in the Indian sweat lodge.

The sweat lodge and the shaman religious leaders give us clues to the fear/power worldview of the Indians. The tradition of honoring or shaming people through honor songs at tribal powwows can help us see the importance of honor and shame in their society. As I have read about Indian culture and history and as I have interacted with missionaries working among North American Indians, I have been amazed at how clearly these cultural traits are part of everyday life.

Likewise, Hinduism and Shintoism are mixtures of shame/honor and fear/power paradigms. Even Russian culture is a mixture, one part being the shame/honor worldview of the east and the Eastern Orthodox Church, and the fear/power worldview of communism.

Clash of Cultures

In many cases, when guilt/innocence cultures have contacted shame/honor cultures they have clashed. As an example, the white man in North America could not understand and appreciate the North American native perspective on life. In the end, many Indians chose to die rather than face the shame of living on a reservation.

In North America in 1889, a young Paiute prophet known as Wovoka gave a message from his home in the Nevada desert. His disciples sent it to all the Indians across western America. The message from their prophet simply urged the Indians to *"Dance everywhere. Keep on dancing. You must not . . . do harm to anyone. You must not fight. Do right always."* Soon village after village of Sioux began to perform his "Ghost Dance" with its promise of a return to old ways in a world from which whites would have been erased by a flood.

The dancing appalled and frightened whites, and they wired to Washington for protection. Army troops fanned out to round up the Ghost dancers and to settle them on reservations. Among the last to be caught was a group of about 350 Sioux under Big Foot. They were led to a military camp at Wounded Knee Creek where they set up camp under a flag of truce. An incident triggered gunfire. When the firing ended, more than 150 Indians, men, women, and children lay dead. Others fled or crawled off wounded. Chief Red Cloud said of the incident, "We had begged for life, and the white men thought we wanted theirs."

Guilt-based cultural values said that Indians must live on reservations. Fear-based cultural values said that the Ghost Dance would change the situation. Sadly, it ended with a massacre.

It is said that the Nez Perce Indians could boast that since Lewis and Clark first encountered their friendliness in Oregon country, no Nez Perce had ever killed a white man. Even when treaties were broken and settlers crowded into their lands they avoided retaliation. In 1877 they were given thirty days to move to a strange reservation in Idaho. Hoping to escape, they began an epic flight to Canada. They were caught 40 miles from the border.

In this case, shame-based cultural values clashed with guilt-based values. Being cooped up on the reservation was a terrible shame and the ultimate humiliation for Indian chiefs. Leaving the reservation was breaking the law.

In 1878 a band of northern Cheyenne left the reservation to return to their old lands "*where their children could live.*" Overtaken by soldiers, a chief said "We do not want to fight you, but we will not go back." Clearly the shame of living on the reservation was too much for them. As they had broken the law by leaving, and now refused to return, the troops opened fire. Some Indians escaped and continued their journey. They met up with soldiers at Fort Robinson where they faced an ultimatum. "*Go south or go hungry.*" Court records tell us what happened next. "*In the midst of the dreadful winter, with the thermometer 40 degrees below zero, the Indians, including the women and children were kept for five days and nights without food or fuel, and for three days without water. At the end of that time they broke out of the barracks."* Troops hunted them down. They chose death over returning to the shame and humiliation of reservation life. Today many natives still feel the sting of shame. Many have turned to the numbing effects of alcohol, and others have immersed themselves in their native religions as they seek answers to their problem of self-esteem.

Western civilizations have now turned their attention to more global issues. Global travel and trade have forced us into a position of trying to understand people from different cultures.

When researching the material for this book, I became aware of the large number of books in print in the western world that deal with the Muslim or Arab mind. These books exist not only in the religious sector but also in the political and business sectors. Westerners, for whatever reason, struggle when they encounter Arabs and other Muslims. Western businessmen struggle to know how to do business in the Muslim world. Western politicians are often confused and unprepared for the actions and reactions of Muslim leaders. Political misunderstandings and blunders have created hardships and even wars. Even Christian missionaries have not fared any better in their efforts to communicate the Christian message.

Throughout the history of Christian outreach to the Muslim peoples of the world, Christians have faced tremendous struggles in knowing how to clearly communicate the gospel message. Most of the church's efforts at communication have been received like water off a duck's back. The message is proclaimed, and the hearers are completely indifferent, sometimes resistant, and occasionally reacting with hostility.

Over the years, countless misunderstandings have developed between Christians and Muslims. Muslims often view Christians as immoral idolaters and blasphemers holding to old documents of untrustworthy heritage. Many Christians are suspicious of Muslims, viewing them as dangerous, and unpredictable. Some go as far as thinking that all Muslims are violent and oppressive.

The battle lines have been drawn up. Many believers in the Lord Jesus find missionary work to Muslims undesirable, a waste of money and perhaps even offensive.

The secular world has not fared any better. Political tensions and issues create misunderstandings on both sides. Many Muslims view western countries as expansionist and threatening. Many western nations view Muslims as terrorists, and their governments as oppressive. The average western person reacts very negatively to leaders such as Ayatollah Khomeini, Muammar al-Qaddafi and Saddam Hussein. Oil-rich Arabs are viewed as a threat to the economic stability of the west. Desperately poor and oppressed Arabs, such as the Palestinians are looked upon as terrorists. On a political level, Muslim nations and western nations have fared no better than Muslim and Christian clerics in understanding one another.

And so over the years, there has been a desire on the part of many westerners to try to understand the Arab Muslim mind. This is why there are many books and articles currently in print on the topic of the Arab mind.

Everyone realizes the importance of this topic. A St. Louis Post dispatch revealed some of the US military thinking when it stated *"Pentagon Threat-Assessment Officer Major Ralph Peters believes intelligence officers must set aside their preoccupation with numbers and weaponry. Instead, he says, they must start reading books that explain human behavior and regional history."*

The religious world has reacted much the same way. Theologians from all backgrounds are now crying out for a greater effort at understanding each other's view points, and for a renewed effort in accepting one another's views.

The problem of understanding one another is not easy. When we meet another person whose system of beliefs is different, we tend to interpret that system according to our own framework of understanding. It can take months and even years of living in another culture to begin to understand that culture. But not everyone reaches a point of understanding. Many westerners living in an Arab culture simply define the culture around them according to their own understanding and perspectives. They assume that the other person thinks in a similar pattern as they do. They then try to understand the culture from their own framework, based on how their own culture works. Years ago, I started out this way, but soon realized that I could not fit everything into neat packages. There was something about Arab society that I did not understand.

My wife and I entered the Arab culture when I was a twenty two year old student. At that point I had read most of the books in print about Arab culture and thought patterns. My move into Arab culture was not so much a conscious decision to understand them, as it was a conscious decision to become part of their culture. I initially concentrated on language learning and cultural adaptation. I began by living among the Arabs in the Levant. After two years, I moved to the edge of the Empty Quarter, and then, one year later, back to the Levant. Several years later, we moved to what was then the Yemen Arab Republic. Many years later, I returned to the Levant, and made my home there until recently. Over the years, we have spent 14 years immersed in Arab culture, and seven years living in western countries, but still close to our Arab friends.

I say this, not to brag of any accomplishments, but rather to point out that our personal experience with the Arab world is based on a wide variety of exposures over a long period of time. Along with our personal experience, we have cultivated friendships with foreigners and nationals living in a host of other Muslim countries, stretching from North Africa to Indonesia.

During our years in the Middle East, I was involved in various types of employment, and I mixed with all levels of society. I have visited the marble palaces of oil-rich Arab sheiks. I have sat in the tents of the poorest Bedouin Arabs. I worked for a number of years as a liaison officer for a western organization, interacting with all levels of government in the Yemen Arab Republic. In the Levant, I worked with charities reaching out to the poor and handicapped. As a rule, we have always made our home in lower middle income neighborhoods.

And in all cases, we have tried to understand and communicate our beliefs to those around us so that they could better understand us, our religion and the society we came from.

One of my initial personal goals was to discover how the Arab mind worked. And so, with my western training ingrained in my thinking, I started asking, "What is going on now?" That seemed to be my favorite question, and for many years I was curious to know what was going on in my neighborhood, in my city and in my nation. I even wanted to know what was going on in my neighbor's head.

During all of these years, I began to notice patterns emerging. The oil-rich Arabs of the gulf, the mountain people of Yemen, the Bedouin of the desert, and the city dwellers of the Levant all held similar codes of conduct. While each region had its peculiarities, there was an overall pattern of similarity between the cultures.

These patterns, however, were not always clearly noticeable. Often there were many confusing and seemingly contradictory events. It was hard to work out what was happening, but in time, I moved on from trying to understand what was happening, to trying to understand why what was happening was happening. I refused to believe that people acted and reacted unpredictably. In fact, the longer I lived in the Arab world, the more I recognized the predictability of the Arabs. During the Gulf war years, I was in the west, and I enjoyed being able to predict certain events in the war, days and sometimes weeks before they happened. However, I found the Gulf war tremendously stressful. Watching western news, I could understand the actions and re-actions of the western nations. Having lived in the Middle East, I could understand the actions and re-actions of the Arab nations. On one side was western understanding, and on the other was Muslim understanding, and in the middle was the yawning chasm of misunderstanding. And countless millions of people paid the price with their lives, their wounds, and tremendous economic loss.

It was during this time that I began to realize how far apart western and Muslim thinking patterns really were. The west saw events and interpreted them one way. The Arabs saw events and interpreted them another way. It wasn't that one was right and the other was wrong. Thinking in terms of right versus wrong is a western thought pattern. During the Gulf war, western governments poured their resources into proving to their people that they were on the side of right, and that Saddam Hussein was on the side of wrong. Numerous instances were relayed to the western public to prove the *wrongness* of the Iraqis' leaders. The people of the west watched their TV's and interpreted the news according to rightness and wrongness, with the majority supporting their government's actions.

In the Middle East, the situation was less clear. Many Arab nations initially supported Saddam Hussein, and only in the face of tremendous western pressure did they start to withdraw their support. Almost all of my Arab friends told me that Saddam Hussein acted predictably and strove manfully to protect his honor and the honor of his nation. Not one of them ever discussed the rightness or the wrongness of the war.

And so, it was during the Gulf war, and in the period since then, that I seriously started to study the Arab Muslim mind, and what it was that made this mindset so different from my own. During this process, I also wrestled with the concept of cross-cultural communication. My role in the Middle East has always been that of a cross-cultural communicator of the Christian Gospel. I have always sought for ways to clearly present the message and teachings of the Christian church as found in the Bible.

As I wrestled with Muslim thought patterns, I began to question my own culture. How did we develop our own thought patterns? Were they right? Is my own culture 'balanced' in its view of life on planet earth? During the course of history, what forces have molded my own culture? I spent many hours studying history in order to understand how events in history molded our western thinking and also Muslim thinking.

Eventually I arrived at conclusions that have been helpful in aiding me in communicating the Gospel of Jesus Christ to those with a Muslim mindset. As I have only just begun down this road, I cannot claim that this material is relevant for every Muslim in every setting. The majority of my experience has been with Arabs. I do not claim to understand the Muslims of Indonesia, China or India. However, since Arabia was the birthplace of Islam, and since Muslim missionaries carried their culture with them, I have found that much of what I have discovered in the Middle East applies to Muslims in other locations.

Having said this, I also realize that Islam is changing, and that western cultures around the world are putting pressure on Islamic culture to change. Islam in the west is struggling to find bridges between western cultural norms and the Muslim mindset. In my interaction with Muslim clerics in Britain and North America I have been amazed at their reinterpretation of certain verses in the Qur'an. These Muslim clerics have arrived at these new interpretations because new interpretations are necessary if Islam is to have any real impact on western guilt-based society.

In the next two chapters we will look at shame and honor in Arab Muslim culture. In doing this, I will not deal with the typical parts of Muslim culture that are often addressed. I will not dwell on *"how much coffee goes into the coffee cup"* nor *"how many times it should be served."* We will not look at body language, rules of etiquette, nor the unspoken rules of the desert. These are all part of culture, and vary from setting to setting. In these chapters, however, I want to go deeper and look at the basic fundamental mindset of Muslims. I want to examine the issues that are most important to the Muslim mind, and upon which cultural rules are built.

CHAPTER NINE

Islam and Shame

"Arab society is a shame-based society," says Dr. Sania Hamady, an Arab scholar and one of the greatest authorities on Arab psychology. "There are three fundamentals of Arab society," she goes on to state, "shame, honor and revenge."

A few years ago, Arabs were loath to talk about their culture. Most Arab people had never interacted with outsiders to the degree that they would start to examine their own and the others' cultures. But that has changed and today you will find Arab psychologists and Arabic media speaking out about their own culture. There are a number of issues that they raise as being important to them.

Group Mindset

Arabs have always lived in groups and they tend to do everything from a group mindset. The larger extended family makes up one's group, and the gathering of all of one's relatives makes up the tribe.

In the cultures I have moved in, Arabs have defined their relationships with others in terms of near and far. Those who are related to you by blood are near, and those from other tribes are far. People can be brought into a near relationship through marriage, or adoption. If a foreigner is adopted as a 'son of the tribe' a great honor has been placed upon him.

Arabs usually demand a high degree of conformity from those who are near to them. This conformity brings honor and social prestige and a secure place in society. The individual who conforms to the group has the advantage that all those members of his group are bound to help his interests and they will defend him unquestioningly against 'outsiders.' I go into this in more detail in the book *Tools for Muslim Evangelism*.

Relationships

From top to bottom Arab society is permeated by a system of rival relationships. This is because in the Arab value system, great value and prestige are placed on the ability to dominate others. In the constant struggle to dominate and to resist domination, the rivals of a given group quickly seize on any 'shame' to destroy the other group's influence. Isolating a target, and thereby destroying it, often achieved this, as an individual could not survive in the desert outside of the group setting. If one tribe attacks the honor of another tribe, the entire tribe will respond, in order to protect their place of honor.

Arabs fear isolation because an individual or small group can only function effectively when he or it is identified with a group or a large body that can offer protection. This fear of isolation can be attributed to the fear that the Bedouins had of being isolated and left as individuals or small groups to fend for themselves in the harsh, hostile desert environment. The isolated persons could easily be taken as a slave by other tribes and could spend the rest of their life in a low and mean position. By sticking together, individuals could offer each other protection. Thus family units and relationships became paramount in knowing whom you could trust, and who would stand by you if an outside force attacked you. Proverbs 14:28 shows similar thinking when it states: *"A large population is a king's glory, but without subjects a prince is ruined."*

Shame

There are many types of shame in an Arab society. For the Arab, failure to conform is damning and leads to a place of shame in the community. This is often hard for Westerners to understand. We in the west value our individualism, but Arabs value conformity. The very meaning of Islam is to conform to the point of submission. The very object of public prayers and universal fasting is to force conformity on all. There is an Arab proverb that can be translated as "*Innovation is the root of all evil.*" If one fails to conform, he is initially criticized, and if he refuses to conform is put in a place of shame by the community.

Shame can also be brought on by an act. Raping one's sister is considered by all as a shameful act. However, few things are considered right or wrong. Right and wrong in Islam are defined by the Qur'an. Something may be right or wrong, because the Qur'an says so. But the Qur'an doesn't provide a nice list of rights and wrongs. So Muslims often talk about society. Society dictates what is acceptable and unacceptable. If you act against society, you may be acting shamefully, but not necessarily wrongfully in God's eyes. After all, the Qur'an tells them that God created good and evil.

Muslim men use this rationalization when living in what they consider an immoral western nation. They can partake in drinking alcohol and sexual escapades, because the society they are living in doesn't define this as shameful. Something may be shameful at home, but when in different circumstances, the Arab may react differently. There is a proverb that states, "*Where you are not known do what ever you like.*"

Beyond this, shame is not only an act against the accepted system of values, but it can also include the discovery, by outsiders, that the act has been committed. Dr. Hamady puts it this way: "He who has done a shameful deed must conceal it, for revealing one disgrace is to commit another disgrace." There is an Arab proverb that says, "*A concealed shame is two thirds forgiven.*"

A Syrian scholar, Kazem Daghestani, tells of an Arab husband who caught his wife in bed with another man. He drew a gun and pointed it at the couple while addressing the man. 'I could kill you with one shot but I will let you go if you swear to keep secret the relationship you have had with my wife. If you ever talk about it I will kill you.' The man took that oath and left and the husband divorced his wife without divulging the cause. He was not concerned about the loss of his wife or her punishment but about his reputation. Public shaming and not the nature of the deed itself or the individual's feelings had determined his action.

The story is told of a sheik who was asleep under the palm tree when a very poor Arab saw him and stole his expensive cloak. In the morning the sheik was angry and his followers hunted down the thief and brought him to trial. When asked for an explanation, the accused said, "Yes, I did steal this cloak. I saw a man asleep under a tree, so I had sexual relations with him while he slept and then I took the cloak. The sheik immediately replied "That is not my cloak," and the thief went free.

The possibility of failure in some way also fills Arabs with dread, as failure leads to shame. So often an Arab will shrink from accepting challenges or responsibilities. However, when away from his family this can change drastically. A meek Lebanese businessman at home can become a shrewd risk taker in the middle of Africa.

When there is failure, often outside forces are blamed. Anger, resentment, and violence are focused on outside elements in order to shift the blame to them. In the case of other Orientals with similar shame/honor type cultures, failure is often focused on the individual, and, for example, a Japanese businessman may take his life when faced with tremendous shame. In an Arab situation, the Arabs will assign blame to someone else and react violently towards him.

As a result, it is very easy to unintentionally offend an Arab. The Arabs have a very detailed code of conduct, and breaking that code can result in offense. This can be as simple as pouring too much coffee, or making your visit too short.

Shame can also result when an Arab is not treated as a special case. He expects any rule to be bent to suit his convenience. He expects to be the favorite, and his friends have to constantly assure him that he counts more than others. For example, when interviewing a number of businessmen, each interview should be conducted exactly the same length of time. Once a man accused an interviewer of spending five more minutes with the previous man. The interviewer got out of the situation by explaining that the extra time was necessary because the previous man could not express himself as eloquently and therefore took longer.

There are lots of little things in Arab culture that matter greatly. Everything in the culture has meaning and an action as simple as stretching the left hand towards a person's face, as a westerner might do in casual gesticulation, could be tantamount to telling many Arabs that he has the evil eye and that your hand was used defensively against it.

It is important to realize that shame is not attached to all of the actions that we would call wrong. While raping one's sister is a very shameful act, things like lying can be either shameful or honorable, depending on the circumstances.

Al Ghazali, the medieval Muslim theologian stated: *"Know that a lie is not wrong in itself, but only because of the evil conclusions to which it leads the hearer, making him believe something that is not really the case. Ignorance sometimes is an advantage, and if a lie causes this kind of ignorance it may be allowed. It is sometimes a duty to lie . . . if lying and truth both lead to a good result, you must tell the truth, for a lie is forbidden in this case. If a lie is the only way to reach a good result, it is allowable. A lie is lawful when it is the only path to duty . . . We must lie when truth leads to unpleasant results, but tell the truth when it leads to good results."*

The rule for telling the truth, or not, is bound by honor and shame. If shame can be avoided, or honor obtained; then lying is more honorable, and therefore the thing to do.

Arabic Words for Shame

The most common Arabic world for shame is *'ayb'*. It is used repeatedly in child raising and usually means "Shame on you." In most cases it is not applied to very young children, because it implies a degree of prior knowledge and instruction that should have been followed. Older children who have disobeyed or have behaved disrespectfully are usually given a lecture which begins and ends with *"ayb"*

The instruction about shame is not restricted to just relatives. Almost anyone can instruct children, telling them that what they are doing is shameful, and usually the children will respond positively, not negatively. The power of the negative use of shame enforced positive reactions in people's lives. Children learn very early on that their personal behavior represents a part of the whole of family honor. Once this sense of honor is acquired, it remains with the person throughout life.

When adults relate together, shame also plays a role. Foul language is undignified and shameful. Losing your temper and shouting insults are shameful. Failing to come to the aid of a family member, or neighbor when one is able and worthy, is shameful. Failing to support family members for whom one is responsible is shameful. Gossip that could or does cause harm is shameful. Anything that adversely and unfairly affects the dignity of another person is considered shameful.

Sometimes when greeting an Arab and asking 'How are you?' one gets the *answer 'mastur al-hal'* or "the condition is covered." This means, everything is all right, and my family and I are not being shamed. All shame is covered.

There is also an Arab word *'hishma'* which means shame or timidity and reserve, often because the person is in a lesser situation. This would strip the Arab of spontaneity and liberty of action while in the presence of someone with greater honor.

Shaming someone with language

There are many ways that Arabs shame and abuse one another with language.

A common form of abuse among women quarrelling over reputations is "*qahba ya bint l'haram* (you slut, you daughter of sin).

A man may be called a *qawwad*, a man who combs the streets looking for johns to bring to a prostitute. This term is perhaps the lowest form of abuse, from one man to another.

More commonly Arabs may angrily say to one another: *May God make your face ugly*, or *May God make your face black*. The inferred meaning is: "May God bring shame upon you."

Calling someone a dog is a great shame, especially calling him a dog in public, since dogs eat scraps and leftovers and not the prime meat that is reserved for the honorable.

Sometimes other family members are also included in the taunt, saying that someone's mother or other family members were illegitimate.

When Shame happens

In Arab culture, shame must be avoided at all cost. If it strikes, it must be hidden. If it is exposed, then it must be avenged. At all costs, honor must be restored.

The fear of shame among Arabs is so powerful because the identification between the individual and the group is far closer than in the west. Because Arabs think in a group mindset, the importance of the group weighs heavier than the importance of an individual. If an individual is in a position of shame, he then looses his influence and power and through him his entire group will similarly suffer, perhaps to the point of destruction.

Revenge

Shame can be eliminated by revenge. This is sanctioned by the Qur'an (sura Xl,173). *"Believers, retaliation is decreed for you in bloodshed."*

It may also be eliminated through payment by fellow kinsmen in the group, or by the public treasury. In the case of a killing, the price of the blood must be settled between whatever groups are involved.

This need for revenge is as strong today as it ever was. In Egypt in 1972, out of 1,120 cases of murder, it was found that 25 percent of the murders were based on the urge to 'wipe out shame.' 30 percent on a desire to satisfy 'wrongs' and another 30 percent on blood-revenge.

In the small country of Jordan, honor killings (killings to preserve honor) have come to public attention. The Jordanian penal code in the 1950's stated: *"He who discovers his wife or one of his female relatives committing adultery and kills, wounds or injures one or both of them is exempt from any penalty."* Some years later a penalty of one year imprisonment was instituted as many murders were being classified as honor killings.

In January 2000 the Jordanian government rejected a bill that would increase the punishment for someone who commits murder because of protecting the honor of the family from one year to life imprisonment. So, in the opening months of 2000, members of the royal family in Jordan joined a demonstration of young Arabs protesting the laws and attitudes about honor killings. Growing numbers of Jordanian young people are educated in the west and western thinking and culture is beginning to clash with traditional eastern thinking and culture.

Peace

In traditional Arab culture, peace is a secondary value, when compared to the degree of feelings that shame and revenge invoke.

This has led to the Western impression that peace in the Arab context is merely the temporary absence of conflict.

In Arab tribal society, where Arab values originated, strife was the normal state of affairs because raiding was one of the two main supports of the economy. In the past, the ideal of permanent peace in Islam was restricted to the community of Islam and to those non-Muslims who accepted the position of protected persons and paid tribute to Islam. On the other hand, Islam instituted jihad (holy war) as the accepted relationship with non-Muslim states, and made no provision for peace with them as sovereign states. Only a truce was permissible, and that was not to last for more than ten years.

This form of thinking then influences all aspects of life. As it has commonly been stated: *"There is honor within Islam, shame without."*

CHAPTER TEN

Islam and Honor

"Honor is understood in a complex way as the absence of shame, for honor and shame are bound to one another as complementary, yet contradictory ideas."

Carolyn Fluehr-Lobban, Islamic Values and Social Practice
1994

The other side of shame is honor, and every Arab desires and strives to be and become more honorable. The relationship between shame and honor has long been recognized by sociologists of Arab and Muslim cultures and also attributed to the generalized Mediterranean social complex.

In many cases the absence of shame conveys the idea of honor. Many times I have heard Arabs describe their families as being honorable, because they don't do or act as others might. Conforming to social mores is utmost to maintaining one's honor.

Honoring Elders

Arab storytellers tell the story of a father who is working in the hot sun with two of his sons. When he needed a drink of water, he asked the older of the boys to get him some. 'No, I will not,' the elder son replied. The father then asked his younger son who said 'Yes, certainly father.' but he did not get the water. At this point the storyteller always asks his audience, "Which is the better son?" To give the wrong answer would be shaming but the storyteller knows that his listeners will give the correct answer. The younger son is the better of the two because he had saved his father's face by not defying him.

In the west we would point out that both boys were wrong. This seems irrelevant to the Arab who does not think in terms of right and wrong, but in terms of shame and honor. To say no to your father's face would be to dishonor him. To agree with him, while in front of him, is to honor him. When Jesus told a similar story in Matthew 21:28-32, he added that the first son, who refused later, went and did what he first refused. In this way, he restored honor by obeying his father. Jesus used this illustration to show that repentance covers shame, and it is very useful in illustrating the need for repentance, not just for wrong deeds, but for shameful deeds.

Honorable acts

If there are shameful acts in the Arab culture, then what are the honorable ones?

In most Muslim cultures, hospitality is one of the most important ways of showing honor. Hospitality honors the guest and covers up any shame the host may have. When you visit an Arab home, great effort is made to be hospitable. Rather than shame you, Arabs try very hard to honor you with hospitality. Everything is done to honor the guest and to present an honorable image of the Arab family.

The reverse is also true. If you don't want someone to visit you, simply talk to him or her outside your door, where everyone will see that they are not invited inside. They will immediately feel shamed and will not return to your home.

If hospitality is first, then flattery must be second in the Arab ways of honoring someone. Arabs are often quick to flatter people they suspect as being honorable. It is a way of pouring extra honor onto a person while demonstrating to others around that they are honoring that person.

Third on my list is gift giving. If you admire something in an Arab home, they will be quick to insist that you have it as a gift. Even if you do not admire something, they will offer you gifts, demonstrating their willingness to honor someone else with a gift.

As the above three demonstrate, a visit to an Arab home is full of expressions of honor. Where you sit in the room, how you are fed, what you are fed, the hospitality shown, the flattery expressed and the gifts that are offered all express various levels of honor. Moreover, the reverse is true. If someone visits your home, you are obliged to be warm and hospitable. It is even expected that you will be overly hospitable almost demanding in your insistence that your guests eat, drink and accept your gifts. You must insist that people eat your food. Small friendly fights break out over the food, and the guests must demonstrate their willingness to accept the hospitality that is shown.

There are many other ways in which honor is calculated in an Arab society:

Honor is attached to your family and your history

As long ago as 1377, Ibn Khaldun wrote: *"One feels shame when one's relatives are treated unjustly or attacked, and one wishes to intervene between them and whatever peril or destruction threatens them."* Also, *"The affection everybody has for his allies results from the feeling of shame that comes to a person when one of his neighbors, relatives or a blood relation in any degree is humiliated."*

An Arab proverb states: *"Learn as much of your pedigrees as is necessary to establish your ties of kindred."* Another adds: *"Many a trick is worth more than a tribe."*

This is the reason that Arabs strive so hard to maintain the honor of the tribe. It is the duty of the eldest son of each family to maintain the honor of the family. If someone greatly offends the tribe, he will be the one to oust them, or, in the case of irreparable damage, execute them.

No where is the honorable status of family and tribe more evident than in the differences between religious beliefs. During the Yemeni War (1962-1965), two Egyptians, a Coptic Christian and a Muslim, both members of well known and upper class families, had been lifelong friends. They were wounded in the same action, the Muslim in the arm and the Copt in the leg. Disabled, they lay awaiting treatment and removal from the battlefield. A half-empty truck arrived and picked up the Muslim, but left the Christian despite his desperate pleas for help. The truck crew had orders to collect the Muslim wounded before the Christian wounded. One word from the wounded Muslim friend could have saved the Copt. It was never uttered, and the Coptic Christian died on the field, probably slaughtered by Yemeni tribesmen.

Education

Education bestows honor. If a man gains a doctorate degree, he receives a great deal of honor in an Arab society. It is for this reason that Arabs strive to gain high educational standing. Many poor families sacrifice almost everything and work very hard to help an elder son make it through higher education. The elder son will work hard to honor the family. In the end, his achievements will raise the entire status of the family, and ultimately of the tribe.

Marriage

A young man has little status in his family until he is married. Suddenly he gains status. Once his first son is born, his status rises even farther. An Arab proverb *states "A man's wife is his honor."* While this sounds like a compliment, the opposite is true. If a man's honor is injured through his wife's misbehavior, swift judgement will come upon her.

Honor in the Arabic language

Language is always changing. That is why the language that a people speaks often reflects the values of the culture.

Albert Hourani, one of the greatest modern Arab scholars living in the West, has said that his people are more conscious of their language than any people in the world. This consciousness is obsessive. Language is everything to the Arab. It is a divine expression. It separates those who are near and far. It separates the educated from the uneducated. It is an art form, and for centuries was the sole medium of artistic expression. Every tribe had its poets, and their unwritten words 'flew across the desert faster than arrows', and, in the midst of outward strife and disintegration, they provided a unifying principle. Poetry gave life and currency to the idea of Arabian virtue. Based on tribal community of blood and insisting that only ties of blood were sacred, poetry became an invisible bond between diverse clans, and formed the basis of a larger sentiment. It was poetry, the ultimate Arab art form, which bound Arabs together as a people, rather than a collection of warring tribes.

When a poet appeared in an Arab family, neighboring tribes gathered together to wish the family joy. There would be feasts, and music. Men and boys would congratulate one another, for a poet was a defense to the honor of them all, a weapon to ward off insult from their good name, and a means of perpetuating their glorious deeds and of establishing their fame forever.

It is interesting to note that traditionally Arabs only wish one another joy, on three occasions: The birth of a boy, the coming to light of a poet, and the foaling of a noble mare.

The Arabic language is so powerful, that Arabs will listen intently to someone speaking well, whether he speaks the truth or not. "*I lift my voice to utter lies absurd, for when I speak the truth, my hushed tones scarce are heard.*" Abu 'lAla, Syrian poet 973-1057

Anyone wanting to understand Arab history and culture must be a student of Arab poetry. Arab poetry is full of vainglory. The poets glorified themselves, their brilliant feats, their courage and resolution and their contempt of death. The Arab hero is defiant and boastful and when there is little to lose, he will ride off unashamed, but he will fight to the death for his women.

An example of the ideal Arab hero, is Shanfara of Azd. He was an outlaw, swift runner, and excellent poet. As a child, Shanfara was captured by the Bani Salman tribe and brought up among them. He did not learn of his origin until he was grown up. He then vowed vengeance against his captors and returned to his own tribe. He swore that he would slay a hundred men of the Beni Salman and he had slain ninety-eight when he was caught in an enemy ambush. In the struggle, one of his hands was hewn off by a sword stroke, but taking the weapon in the other, he flung it in the face of the Salman tribesman and killed him, making his score ninety-nine. He was then overpowered and slain. As his skull lay bleaching on the ground, a man of his enemies passed by and kicked it. A splinter of bone entered his foot, the wound festered and he died, thus completing Shanfara's hundred.

Arabic words for Honor

Honor is a value that is applied to both individuals and families or tribes. "*Sharaf*" is a quality that all desire. "*Sharif*" is a man's name, meaning honor. "*Shariifa*" is a woman's name, meaning honorable.

When guests arrive at your door, you can respond, "*Itsharafna*" (You honor us), and the response of the guest is "*Itsharaft nehna*" "We are honored."

Sharaf goes much deeper than good manners. Honor embodies the pride and dignity that a family possesses due to its longstanding good reputation in the community for producing upright men and women who behave themselves well, marry well, raise proper children, and above all, adhere to the principles and practice of their religion. An honorable family produces sons who are *shariifs*, and daughters who are *ashraaf*.

The Arabic word *'ird* deals with reputation; what other people think. This reputation is more important than fact. If a man from one group approaches a woman, and is rebuffed, but later brags about it, perhaps even adding lies, the woman's group will be forced to punish her and thus themselves. The offence against *'ird* becomes very serious when public notice is taken. This is why Arab women fear being alone with a man. If there are no witnesses, the man can say anything about their time together, and the woman will bear the consequences.

Arabs can have different values when it comes to *'ird*. For example, one's reputation regarding the women of his tribe may outweigh his honor as a fighter. Often *'ird* is used in the plural sense. *Shirridna bi'irdna*, a common proverb among the men means *"We came away with our honor intact."*

It is also interesting to note that the Arabic word for *ask* and *tell* is exactly the same word. I don't *ask*, I *tell* you to loan me something, because it would be unthinkable for you to refuse me, as this would be a shame. In much the same way, if someone has it in their power to help someone else, (especially if they are related) they must. Not to do so would be a shame to the whole tribe. Even if a person disagrees, the claim of the tribe is greater than his own opinions.

What makes a person honorable?

I have asked this question to many Arabs. If they are confused, then I clarify the question by asking, what makes a person honorable enough to be a sheik? What would you look for in a person, before you would vote for him to be your sheik? The answers are interesting.

Money

Arabs have a tremendous respect for wealth. Down through history, most honorable Arab leaders have been wealthy ones. Even Mohammed, the founder of Islam, rose to a position of great wealth. The use of this wealth, to help the poor and the masses, is seen as very honorable, and is often portrayed in Arabic literature and stories. Wealth allows the leader to be hospitable and generous, two elements that are extremely useful in obliterating shame and restoring honor. A wealthy leader can throw money around, gaining respect, and covering a multitude of sins.

Heritage

Arabs are keenly aware of their heritage. Some can trace their heritage back to Mohammed. Others back to great leaders. Every tribe has stories of how individuals in their tribe achieved great honor or displayed honorable characteristics. Shameful figures in the tribal background are expelled or killed in order to preserve the tribe's honorable heritage.

Wisdom

Arabs respect age and wisdom. Elders are listened to with respect. The language elders use is often more formal and elevated than young people are capable of. Elders are looked to for their wisdom, as they know all the old stories and can often give wise and good counsel. Elders often have more money, and may have demonstrated their wisdom in acquiring riches, or maintaining the tribal lands and tribal honor.

Charisma

Certain individuals have charisma. They are good looking, have a confidence about them, and carry themselves with honor. Often they have accomplished something of note and have been able to capitalize on it. Many times they are good at communication and at politically finding honorable solutions to problems.

Physical Strength

Arab lore is full of heroes who display tremendous physical strength. Most Arab boys are brought up to think highly of being manly and strong. Physical strength, as well as charisma and financial strength are a winning combination in Arab culture.

Alliance

Many Arabs look to leaders who have formed strong alliances. Since strength and riches are often found in a group setting, someone with strong alliances can rely on the combined strengths of many groups. Many political leaders in the Arab world use their alliances with tribes and families to put them into political power.

Bravery

Every Arab boy knows stories of Arab heroes who faced overwhelming odds. Whether he overcame or not is not the issue. The act of bravery, in itself, is very honorable. If one sits in an Arab coffeehouse and listens to the storytellers, or if you visit your neighbors and ask, you will hear stories of brave Arab heroes.

Loyalty

All Arabs belong to a group or tribe. Loyalty to the family tribe is considered paramount to maintaining honor. One does not question the correctness of the elders or tribes in front of outsiders. It is paramount that the tribe sticks together in order to survive. Once again, Arab history and folklore are full of stories of heroes who were loyal to the end.

Violence

Dr. Sania Hamady, one of the greatest authorities on Arab psychology, herself an Arab, says: "life is a fearful test, for modern Arab society is ruthless, stern and pitiless . . . It honors strength and has no compassion for weakness."

In Arab countries between 1948 and 1973, a mere quarter of a century, no fewer than eighty revolts occurred, most of them bloody and violent. No wonder the west has a negative view of Arabs and Islam.

Violence, in Arab history, has been part of demonstrating one's honor, and in removing shame from the tribe. *"With the sword will I wash my shame away. Let God's doom bring on me what it may!"* Abu Tammam, a ninth-century poet in Hamasa.

You can see from the list of characteristics above why Arabs have a hard time recognizing Jesus as an honorable person. He did not display the usual characteristics that identify a person of honor. There is, however, one more characteristic of honor, that Jesus exemplified. Some Arab heroes demonstrated their honor by reaching down, and helping people in need; people who didn't deserve it.

If Jesus' character becomes an issue in your discussion, then one needs to share about servant leadership, and how Jesus displayed incredible honor, by reaching down into our situation to help us, and honor us.

Before we criticize Middle Eastern culture for their views on honor and shame, we must admit that our own history, only a few short hundred years ago, was rife with honor and shame. The 'high' French and German culture of the 18th and 19th century gave rise to dueling, which carried over to the gun fighters of the American west. In Europe, a culture of honor survived for many years among the military and military families. These events are often forgotten, as we tend to view history through the filter of our own experience.

Conclusion

Honor in an Arab society is understood, in a complex way, as the absence of shame. Honor and shame are diametrically opposed factors, and the fundamental issue that defines society. In most shame/honor-based societies, people accept that everyone has to deal with a measure of shame. The question is, "how is shame dealt with?" Few families or tribes can escape the birth of a handicapped child. The question then arises, what should be done with this child? Should the child be hidden away? Should it be killed? Should it be neglected, so that it eventually goes away? Is it more humane to quietly give it to an institution?

In some shame/honor-based cultures, Christian societies have reached out to handicapped children in crisis, attempting to rescue them from families that are reeling from the shame of having birthed such a child. Sometimes handicaps are not so easily noticed. The child grows, and becomes a part of the family fabric. Then disaster falls, when it becomes increasingly obvious that the child is deaf, or has some other handicap that was not immediately noticeable. The discovery of such handicaps can crush whole families, as they lose their place of honor in the community.

We came across this in our own family situation. Our eldest son has cerebral palsy, and his presence in our family was of particular interest to our friends as they tried to assess what this meant in regards to our honorable status, both in the church and in the community.

The question that always troubled me was, "can a person move from a position of shame to a position of honor?" Arabs have more trouble with this one. Almost all agree that someone can honor you but you cannot honor yourself. However, people with honor seldom honor others without cause.

This is where we must be bold in proclaiming the gospel. The gospel that Jesus brought, is simply this: God wants to lift man from a position of shame to a position of honor. When Jesus said, "I am the way," this is what he was referring to. Jesus is the only one who can bring us into the presence of God the Father. This is why Jesus had to be God. No one else would do. Only God could reach down to mankind. Jesus Christ was God displayed in the flesh, bringing us the message of reconciliation, a message of hope. God was providing a way to lift us from a place of shame to a place of honor.

CHAPTER ELEVEN

The Three-Fold Message of Salvation

Many times over the years, I have asked myself, "How does one effectively communicate the gospel to Muslim people?" As I have pondered this question, I have broken it down into two questions. First, what is the gospel message, and secondly, how is it best communicated to those who live in a shame-based culture, such as the Muslims of the Middle East?

Review

In order to communicate the gospel to all cultures and worldviews, we need to accept that the Bible starts out with three salvation themes: Guilt, Shame and Fear. We in the west have taken the guilt theme and have traced it through the Bible. We have formed our understanding of the gospel and our systematic theology around this theme. In the Garden of Eden, the Bible tells us that Adam and Eve suffered guilt. They knew they were naked, and they sewed fig leaves together to make themselves clothing. From this beginning, we trace God's plan of salvation, to free man from guilt, right through the Bible. This is the standard western way of explaining the gospel.

But the Bible also tells us that Adam and Eve were ashamed and hid themselves. This is the beginning of shame. And the theme of God's dealing with the shame that came on mankind runs throughout the length of the scriptures.

Adam then replied to God that when he heard God's voice in the garden, he was afraid. The theme of God dealing with our fear also runs through the Bible.

So today, these three reactions to Adam and Eve's first act of rebellion form the basis for building worldviews and cultures. Shame and honor form the basis of the cultures that span from Morocco to Japan. It is almost exactly the same area as is covered by the 10/40 window. As our ability to understand shame-based cultures has been so minimal in history, it is no wonder that the church has made little impact on this part of the world.

Fear-based cultures are found among the Animists of the world, in Africa and South America and other areas. Missionaries have worked in these areas for a number of years, and have seen God move, as they ministered God's message of victory over the power of the enemy and release from fear through Jesus Christ. For many years missionaries have shown how God is greater than the witch doctors and the demons that hounded people's lives.

When man sinned, three great conditions came upon mankind. When man broke God's law, he was in a position of guilt. When man broke God's relationship, he was in a position of shame. When man broke God's trust, he was in a position of fear.

Guilt is simply a sense of having done something wrong. This implies a law has been broken. Fear on the other hand, usually implies being afraid of a consequence. You are afraid because of an action or inaction. Shame, on the other hand, is the feeling of embarrassment or a sense of unworthiness, as felt in a relationship between two or more people. Salvation has to do with saving us from God's judgment, restoring our relationship with God, and rebuilding trust and putting power back into the hands of God.

What is the Gospel?

The question that faces us is simply, are there three or more models that we can use to explain the gospel? Should we adopt one model as the method that we use in one setting? When working among guilt-based cultures, should we stick to our legal model of salvation? Do we develop a power model of salvation for use among the fear-based cultures of the world? Is there a special shame/honor model of salvation that we should use among the shame-based cultures of the world? What about cultures that demonstrate combinations of these three? Do we develop other models?

I think not. I don't believe there are separate models of salvation that are to be used in different settings. The Bible gives us no clue that God ever intended this to be. Rather, the three themes of salvation are woven together in the scriptures, to present a complete picture of what God wants to do with mankind.

I believe that any presentation of the gospel, in any culture, should address all three areas of guilt, shame, and fear. Taken together, these present a much clearer picture of God's plan of salvation.

With these three in mind, the missionary should address five different areas:

1. Repentance

This is the act of coming to God and accepting His way over our way. Repentance can be viewed in various forms. It is more than just turning from sin, it is turning from pride (pursuing one's own honor) and accepting what God has done for us. It is also turning from a life of fear to a life where one is trusting in Christ's victory on the cross to defeat the enemy.

2. Sacrifice

Christ's sacrifice on the cross was not only for our sin, but also addresses our shame and our fear. Answers to all three lie in Christ's work on the cross.

3. Redemption

In the western mind, redemption has to do with sin and guilt. In a shame-based culture, redemption has to do with a mediator working out payment to cover shame, and redeem the honor of the tribe. In this case, God has been offended, and a payment must be made to restore the relationship between mankind and God.

4. Propitiation

When the community is offended, it expels the offender in order to maintain a quality of love and acceptance. When God was offended he expelled those who offended him in order to maintain a quality of love and acceptance. If propitiation is the removal of wrath by the offering of a gift, then propitiation can be explained in terms of God's wrath being removed by Jesus' work on the cross. This can be explained in terms of God's laws demanding the guilty be punished, or as God's wrath against us being appeased through the death of Christ on the Cross.

5. Reconciliation

This is the act of restoring the relationship between man and God. It is more than the legal action of removing guilt, it is the act of God bringing us into a personal father/son relationship with Himself. Shame is removed and honor is restored.

Where to start

The secret to sharing the gospel, if there is such, is to use one of the three building blocks as the initial expression of the gospel as it correlates with the worldview of the culture you are dealing with. If you are working in a guilt-based culture, there will be a felt need to deal with guilt. If you are working in a shame-based culture, there is a felt need to address shame. The same goes for a fear-based culture, needing to address fear.

The tactics of the church must change, depending on the culture that is being addressed. We have done an excellent job in communicating to the western world that the church offers God's forgiveness for sin. There is a general vague awareness among most western people that this is to be the role of the church.

In an eastern setting, the church needs to communicate the message that God is offering hope to those in a position of shame.

In a fear-based culture, the church must communicate the message that God offers freedom from the bondage of fear.

In every case, however, we must not limit our message to just the one facet. As I have traveled in North America, I have tried to concentrate my preaching around the fact that God not only offers forgiveness of sins, but He also offers freedom from fear, and a lifting from shame. I have been amazed at the overwhelming response to this message. People have come to me telling me that they have asked for forgiveness for their sins, but they still carried shame. Others are stricken with anxiety and fear. Our focus in the west on guilt has left some of us with only a partial understanding of the gospel. And some Christians are suffering because they are still bound by shame or fear.

We who communicate the gospel message must share the full three-fold message of salvation. It is like a braided chord or rope. The three parts wrap around each other, strengthening each other.

All three should be present in our Gospel presentation. Which one will be our starting point in sharing the gospel, will depend on which culture we live in.

In an animistic culture, it is natural to begin our message of salvation with something that focuses on fear. Man fears because man rebelled and did his own thing, and the result of this action is fear. We have a message of hope for those living in a world of animistic fear. This message of salvation would not be complete, however, without animistic people learning to understand that Christ came to remove our guilt, and also that Christ came to lift us from shame. Once someone understands all three views, they have a solid grasp of what Jesus came to do on the cross.

In the same way, those living in shame-based cultures need to have a complete view of salvation, but the door through which they will most easily come, is the one that starts with man's shame in the Garden of Eden. This is the world they understand. But in the same way, they must also understand the full message of salvation, and must deal with their guilt and fears.

Paul was fully aware of this, when he wrote about making the message understood to the Jews, the Greeks, and the barbarians. Even in Paul's day, the world was split into three great worldviews.

The Jews were a Semitic people who lived in a shame-based culture. The Greeks were the ones who were developing a guilt-based culture, and the barbarians were those who lived in fear-based cultures. But Paul did not preach three separate messages of salvation. He preached only one. Paul, however, used different techniques when addressing different people. In his letter to the Romans, he speaks to people who lived in a more or less guilt-based society. In his letter to the Romans, he addresses man's guilt and transgression of man's laws. This is illustrated in our use of the Roman's Road, and the Four Spiritual Laws. When Paul was on Mars Hill, he addressed the Greek's pantheon of gods, drawing their attention to the unknown god and to Christ's resurrection on the cross as demonstrating that there was only one powerful God in the universe. (Acts 17:1-34)

Cross-cultural contextualization of the Gospel is simply knowing how to start the Gospel message from a place of common understanding. It is knowing how to relate the Gospel message in a language and form that as meaningful to its listeners. Finally, it is knowing how to bring the person to a full understanding of Christ's work on the cross.

In many cases, new believers drift away, because they have not grasped a complete picture of salvation. They need a lot of teaching in order to grow, because they have responded to only one of the aspects of salvation, and see the work of Christ on the cross in a very limited way.

It is the responsibility of the person sharing the gospel to address all three aspects of guilt, shame and fear, tracing God's message of salvation throughout the Bible. It is there. It is clearly demonstrated in the Garden of Eden. It is pictured in the various acts of worship in the Temple. It is clearly addressed by the prophets, and is clearly presented in Isaiah 53. The three-fold message of salvation is seen in the cross of Christ. It is present at Pentecost, and is addressed in the believer's ultimate position in heaven.

Often missionaries from guilt-based cultures have busied themselves with pointing out the sins of people living in shame-based cultures. But the people they are addressing never feel guilt. They may feel that the missionary is shaming them by drawing attention to areas of their lives. Missionaries can go even farther, unintentionally shaming people by asking why they weren't in church, and encouraging them to attend. In the end, it may cause them to attend, but it may simply be because they don't want to shame the missionary. Many of our well meaning western ways of ministering can be taken wrongly in another culture.

Mary (not her real name) is a nurse working in a Christian hospital. When she arrived at the hospital, the staff told her that she should not bother to witness to one of the national workers, as they had been witnessing to him for many years, without result. Mary tried her best to share the gospel, but this man, a Muslim, was not interested. Sometime later, Mary attended one of my seminars and became excited about sharing the gospel from a shame/honor perspective. She told me about this man, and how he could not find work, and finally in desperation took the job at a Christian hospital. Some time later, his first child was born, handicapped. Other handicapped children followed. Mary sensed that this man was struggling with a load of shame.

Mary made another visit to this man and his wife. During the visit she asked them if they understood all the things the foreigners had been telling them about guilt and sin. They said no. Then she asked them if they understood shame and honor. Their eyes lit up. Mary said, "Let me tell you about Jesus and what he came to do." For the first time in their lives, this Muslim couple heard a gospel presentation that spoke to their felt needs. Although they didn't accepted Christ at that meeting, the door was opened for repeated visits.

I trust that through the message of this book, you have been challenged to dig deeper and learn more efficiently how to share the gospel with people from other cultures. I have not attempted to explain everything in this book. That would require volumes, and is not necessary at this time. The purpose of this book is simply to unlock the door, and open a world of new understanding when it comes to sharing the gospel with people from other cultures.

3539-GIBS

CHAPTER TWELVE

The Continuing Story

Over the last three thousand years of history, great historical periods have come and gone. In the years before Christ, the world was torn apart by competing armies. The Egyptians, Assyrians, Babylonians, and others vied for power. Vast armies moved back and forth over the known world with first one and then another civilization becoming dominant. Despite their linguistic and cultural differences, most of these civilizations held a similar worldview. Gods and demons controlled their universe, and man lived in fear of these powers, and he did what he could to appease them. The first chapters of civilization on earth were in the hands of those who lived in fear-based cultures.

At the time of Christ, the guilt-based cultures had risen to great power, and they strove to take over the known world. First Greek and then Roman armies marched across the world, seeking to subject everyone to their worldview. While their civilizations still had many fear-based qualities, their new emphasis on the law helped them develop the first great civilizations based on using guilt as a controlling factor. The millenium following the birth of Christ belonged to these guilt-based cultures. These civilizations were known as the Greek, Roman and Byzantine Empires.

In the last days of the year 999, civilization was following a clear course. The future of world politics lay with Islam. It was an unstoppable force that would eventually control much of the known world, including whatever parts of Europe they chose to occupy.

The Muslims had energy, confidence, and imagination. Their society was now far superior to that in Europe. Bernard Lewis, the renowned historian of Islam, has written that the Muslims of those days *"(they) neither feared nor respected the barbarous individuals of northern and western Europe, whome they saw as uncouth primitives."* Islam, at this stage was probably the most sophisticated and cosmopolitan civilization in the world.

So how did it happen, that Christian Europe and the colonies it established in America, eventually dominated the world? What started out as Islam's millennium became Europe's in the end. Islam grew until 1669, when the Ottoman Empire, after a long war, took Crete from the Venetians. That turned out to be Islam's last acquisition. Fourteen years later it became obvious that history was reversing itself. In 1683, the Ottomans, after trying to conquer Vienna for 60 days, withdrew in disarray. The fighting that followed destroyed much of their army and crippled the military wing of Islam.

A Polish man named Kulyeziski had been instrumental in defending the city, and for his efforts he was rewarded all the coffee the Turkish army left behind. Gifted in the ability to capitalize on opportunity, he opened a cafe in Vienna, and commissioned a baker to create a unique new pastry to accompany the coffee and celebrate the great victory over Islam. The baker produced a crescent shaped pastry that the Viennese could eat to celebrate their devouring of the Muslims. It was called the croissant.

From the Muslim perspective, however, Europe soon ceased to be an invasion target and became an alien force whose armies and cultures began to trespass on Arab lands. A key year in European history was 1492. The date is well known as the year when Columbus arrived in the Americas. In January of that year, however, Granada, the last Islamic city in Spain, surrendered to Christian armies. Before the year was over, Columbus had arrived in America and Europe started their great expansion westward across the Atlantic.

Islam now turned its attention to the shame-based cultures of the east, spreading as far as Indonesia and Malaysia, and deep into China. In the south, they began moving against the fear-based African cultures, spreading deep into Africa.

And so history has moved from the early civilizations that were fear-based (BC), to the rapid expansion of the guilt-based cultures (100 BC—999 AD). During the millenium from 999 AD till 1999, shame-based cultures seem to have had the first opportunity, and then the ball was passed to the guilt-based cultures of America and Northern Europe.

At the end of the second millenium, in 1999, Islam has stopped growing. One of the dominant forces on the face of the earth today is the evangelical church. By the end of 1999, evangelicals were the fastest growing religious force in the world. They have penetrated almost every country of the world and continue rapid growth in many third world countries.

Patrick Johnstone, in his book, *The Church is Bigger than You Think*, tells us that evangelicals are growing at over three times the population rate, and are the world's only body of religious adherents growing rapidly by means of conversion.

The question remains, will the next millenium be ours? Will the church of Jesus Christ be able to relate to all worldviews? All of the great civilizations of the world have failed to move out of their particular worldview with any success. Usually, their own worldview has changed, when brought into confrontation with others.

It was not by mere chance that Jesus was born into a stable in Bethlehem, and that his death on the cross took place in the city of Jerusalem. The cross of Christ stands firmly at the crossroads of history. To the west are the guilt-based cultures of the world. To the south the fear-based cultures, and to the east the shame-based cultures. And in the midst of all of them, the cross of Christ stands as a strong bold message of peace on earth and good will to all mankind.

The church of Jesus Christ has the message and the methods to relate to every worldview and every culture in the world. In this book I have simply attempted to unlock the door to our understanding of guilt-, shame-, and fear-based cultures. It is my hope and desire that soldiers of the cross of Christ will open the door, and with the Bible in one hand, and the Holy Spirit guiding them, will enter into a world that few soldiers of the cross have entered before. The millenium that should have belonged to the shame-based cultures is over, and now it is our turn.

I have simply attempted to unlock the door. It is now your duty, as a servant of the Lord Jesus, to open the door, and discover that the fields are indeed white unto harvest, but the laborers are few. May God bless you, as you labor in his harvest field.

BIBLIOGRAPHY AND
SUGGESTED READING

Abduh, M. *The Theology of Unity*, translated by I. Musa'ad, K. Gregg, (London: Allen and Unwin, 1966)

Abu Lughod, Lila. *Veiled Sentiments; Honor and Poetry in a Bedouin Society* (Los Angeles: University of California Press, 1986)

Ahmad, K. *Family Life in Islam* (Leicester, UK: The Islamic Foundation, 1974)

Ahmad, K. *Islam—Its Meaning and Message* (Islamic Council of Europe, 1975)

Aldrich, Virgil, *An Ethics of Shame* (Ethics, 50 (Oct) 1939) pp. 57-77

Altorki, Soraya and Camillia Fawzi El-Solh, (editors) *Arab Women in the Field: Studying Your Own Society* (Syracuse, New York: Syracuse University Press, 1988)

Antoun, Richard, T. *On the Modesty of Women in Arab Muslim Villages: A study in the Accommodation of Traditions* (American Anthropologist, 70:4 1968) pp. 671-697

Antoun, Richard T. *Arab Village* (Indiana University Press, 1972)

Bagadee, Halid-e, *Belief and Islam* (Istanbul, Turkey, 1973)

Baroja, Julio Caro, *Honor and Shame: A Historical Account of Several Conflicts,* in *Honor and Shame: The Values of Mediterranean Society* (Chicago: University of Chicago Press, 1966) pp. 81-137

Bates, D., and A. Rassam, *People and Cultures of the Middle East* (Englewoods Cliffs, New Jersey: Prentice-Hall, 1983)

Beck, Lois, and Nikki Keddie (editors) *Women in the Muslim World* (Cambridge: Harvard University Press, 1978)

Bediako, Kwame, *Biblical Christologies in the context of African Traditional Religions,* in *Sharing Jesus in the Two Thirds World,* Samuel, Vinay, Sugden, Chris, (editors) (Bangkok 1983)

Benedict, R. The *Chrysanthemum and the Sword: Patterns of Japanese Culture* (Boston: Houghton Mifflin, 1946)

Berger, Morroe, *The Arab World Today* (New York: Doubleday, 1964)

Berkouwer, G. C. *Sin,* Translated by Philip C. Holtrop, (Grand Rapids: Eerdmans, 1971)

Billard, Jules B., (editor) *The World of American Indians* (Washington D.C: National Geographic Society, 1974)

Bourdieu, Pierre, *The Sentiment of Honor in Kabyle Society,* in *Honor and Shame: The Values of Mediterranean Society,* (Chicago: University of Chicago Press, 1966) pp. 192-241

Braithwaite, John, *Crime, Shame and Reintegration* (Cambridge: Cambridge University Press, 1989)

Burnett, David, *Clash of Worlds* (Sussex, UK: MARC, Eastbourne, Monarch Publications, 1990)

Burnett, David, *Unearthly Powers* (Nashville: Oliver-Nelson Books, Thomas Nelson Inc., 1988)

Cairns, Earle, E. *Christianity through the Centuries* (Grand Rapids Mich.: Zondervan Publishing House, 1974)

Campbell, J. K. *Honor, Family and Patronage* (New York, Oxford University Press, 1964)

Capps, Donald, *The depleted self: sin in a narcissistic age* (Minneapolis: Fortress Press, 1993)

Carrington, P., *The Early Christian Church, 2 vols.* (London: Cambridge University Press, 1957)

Clifford, W. *Crime Control in Japan* (Lexington, Mass: Lexington Books, 1976)

Curtis, Michael, (editor), *People and Politics in the Middle East* (New Brunswick, New Jersey: Transaction Inc, 1971)

Doniach, N. S. editor, *The Oxford English-Arabic Dictionary of Current Usage* (Oxford: Oxford University Press, 1984)

Drury, Nevill, *The Elements of Shamanism* (Element Books, Shaftesbury, 1989)

Dudley, Donald R. *The Civilization of Rome* (New York: Mentor Books, New American Library, 1962)

Dwyer, Kevin, *Arab Voices: the Human Rights Debate in the Middle East* (Berkley: University of California Press, 1991)

Eberhard, Wolfram, *Guilt and sin in traditional China* (Berkeley: University of California Press, 1967)

Eberhard, Wolfram, *Social mobility in traditional China* (Leiden, Netherlands: E. J. Brill, 1962)

Esposito, John L. *Women in Muslim Family Law* (Syracuse: Syracuse University Press, 1982)

Fernea, Elisabeth, Warnock, *Guests of the Sheikh: An Ethnography of An Iraqi Village* (New York: Doubleday and Co., 1965)

Fluehr-Lobban, Carolyn, *Islamic Society in Practice* (Gainsville, Florida: University Press of Florida, 1994)

Fluehr-Lobban, Carolyn, *Islamic Law and Society in the Sudan* (London: Frank Cass and Co., London, 1987)

Fulford, Robert, *History's Surprise, Requiem for an Empire* Lost (National Post clipping)

Gellner, Ernest, *Muslim Society* (Cambridge: Cambridge University Press, 1981)

Gibb, H. A. R., and Kramers, J. H. *The Shorter Encyclopaedia of Islam* (Leiden, Netherlands: E. J.Brill, 1953)

Gibbon, Edward, *Decline and Fall of the Roman Empire* (New York: Penguin Books, 1985)

Gilmore, David, *Honor and Shame and the Unity of the Mediterranean* (Washington D.C: Special Publication no. 22 American Anthropological Association, 1987)

Goodwin, Jan, *Price of Honor; Muslim Women Lift the Veil of Silence on the Islamic World* (Boston: Little, Brown and Company, 1994)

Guenther, Ken, *Pain in a Shame Culture: Help for the Filipino Pastor* (Vancouver: Regent College, Unpublished Term Paper, December 1977)

Hamady, Dr. Sania, *Temperament and Character of the Arabs* (New York: Twayne Publishers, 1960)

Harris, George L. *Iraq: Its People, Its Society, Its Culture* (New Haven: Human Relations Area File Press, 1958)

Hiebert, Paul, Shaw, Dan, Tienou, Tite, *Understanding Folk Religion: A Christian's Response to Popular Beliefs and Practices* (Grand Rapids: Baker, 1999)

Hodgkin, E.C. *The Arabs* (Oxford: Oxford University Press, 1970)

Hossein, Seyyed, *The Encounter of Man and Nature* (London: Allen and Unwin, 1968)

Hourani, Albert, *Arabic Thought in the Liberal Age* (Oxford: Oxford Paperbacks, 1970)

Hourani, Albert, *History of the Arabs* (Cambridge: Harvard University Press, 1991)

Hu, Chang-tu, *China: Its People, Its Society, Its Culture* (New Haven: Human Relations Area File Press, 1960)

Hu, Hsien-Chin, *The Chinese Concepts of Face*, in Haring (editor) *Personal Character and Cultural Milieu*, Third Edition, (Syracuse:

Syracuse University Press, 1956) pp. 446-467. Reprinted from the American Anthropologist 46:45-64, 1944

Ibn Khaldun, *The Maqaddimah: An Introduction to History*, (various editions)

Johnston, Patrick, *Operation World* (Cumbria, UK: OM Publishing and WEC International, 1993)

Johnston, Patrick, *The Church is Bigger than You Think* (Pasadena, California: William Carey Library Publishers, 1998)

Kalinowski, Isaiah *The Shame Culture that is Wabash* (Amman Jordan: Jordan Times October 7, 1999) Vol. 107:6

Kamal, Ahmad, *The Sacred Journey* (London: Allen and Unwin, 1964)

Karpat, Kemal H. (editor) *Political and social thought in the Contemporary Middle East* (London, Praeger, New York: Pall Mall Publishing, 1968)

Kraft, Charles H. *Christianity in Culture* (Maryknoll, New York: Orbis Books, 1981)

Krog, Antjie, *Country of My Skull* (Johannesburg: Random House)

Lane, Denis, *One World, Two Minds* (OMF, 1995)

Latourette, Kenneth Scott, *A History of Christianity, Volume I* (New York, London: Harper and Rowe, 1975)

Lawrence, T .E. *The Seven Pillars of Wisdom* (Lawrence of Arabia) (London, 1946)

Le Bar, Frank M. and Suddard, Adrienne (editors), *Laos: Its Society, Its Culture* (New Haven: Human Relations Area File Press, 1960)

Lewis, Bernard, *The Arabs in History* (Hutchinson University Library, 1970)

Lewis, Michael, *Shame: the exposed self* (New York: Free Press; Toronto: Maxwell Macmillan Canada; New York: Maxwell Macmillan International, 1992)

Lingenfelter, Sherwood G. *Transforming culture: a challenge for Christian mission* (Grand Rapids, Mich.: Baker Book House, 1992)

Lowell, L. Nobel, *Naked and Not Ashamed: An Anthropological, Biblical and Psychological Study of Shame* (Jackson, Michigan: Jackson Printing, 1975)

Lyall, Sir Charles *Ancient Arabian Poetry* (1900)

Lynd, Helen Merrel, *On Shame and the Search for Identity* (London: Routledge and Kegan Paul, 1966)

Lystad, Robert A., The *Ashanti: A Proud People* (New Brunswick, New Jersey: Rutgers University Press, 1958)

Maine, Sir. Henry Sumner, *Ancient Law* (Great Britain: Dorset Press, 1861, 1986)

Mattingly, H., *The Man in the Roman* Street (New York: The Numismatic Review, 1947)

Maybury, Richard J. *Ancient Rome: How it affects you today* (Placerville, California: Bluestock Press, 1995)

Maybury, Richard J. *Whatever Happened to Justice?* (Placerville, California: Bluestock Press, 1993)

Mbiti, John, S. *Concepts of God in Africa* (London: SPCK, 1971)

Merrell, Lynd Hellen, *On Shame and the Search for Identity* (New York: Harcourt, 1958)

Miranda, Dionisio M., Buting Pinoy: *Probe Essays on Value as Filipino* (Manila, Philippines: Divine Word Publications)

Mises, Ludwig von, *Theory and History* (Yale University Press, Arlington House, 1957, 1985)

Morrison, Andrew P. *Shame, the underside of Narcissism* (Hillsdale, NJ: Analytic Press, distributed solely by Lawrence Erlbaum Associates, 1989)

Mowrer, O. Hobart, *The Crisis in Psychiatry and Religion* (Princeton: D. Van Nostrand, Insight Book, 1961)

Muller, Roland, *Tools for Muslim Evangelism*, (Belleville, Ontario: Essence Publishing, 2000)

Nicholson, R.A. *A Literary History of the Arabs* (Cambridge: Cambridge University Press, 1929)

Niebuhr, H. Richard, *Christ and Culture* (New York: Harper and Brothers, 1951)

Parrinder, Geoffrey, *African Mythology* (London: Paul Hamlyn, 1967)

Patai, Raphael, *The Arab Mind* (New York: Charles Scribner's Sons, 1973)

Peristiany, J.G. *Honour and Shame in a Cypriot Highland Village*, Honor and Shame: The Values of Mediterranean Society (Chicago: University of Chicago Press, 1966) pp. 173-190

Piers, Gerhart and Singer, Milton, *Shame and Guilt: A Psychoanalytic and Cultural Study* (Springfield, Illinois: Charles C. Thomas, 1953)

Practical Anthropology (Various Issues, 1959–1992)

Ross, Fiona, C. *Culture of Shame to a Circle of Guilt* (Pretoria, South Africa)

Rugh, Andrea B. *Family Life in Contemporary Egypt* (Syracuse: Syracuse University Press, 1984)

Samuel, Vinay, Sugden, Chris, (editors) *Sharing Jesus in the Two Thirds World*, (1983)

Stein, Edward, V., *Guilt: Theory and Therapy* (Philadelphia: Westminster Press, 1968)

Stewart, Frank, Henderson, *Honor* (Chicago: University of Chicago Press, 1994)

Steyne, Philip, M. *Gods of Power* (Houston: Torch Publications, 1990)

Tournier, Paul, *Guilt and Grace: A Psychological Study* (New York: Harper and Row, 1962)

Toynbee, Arnold, *Greek Civilization and Character* (New York & Toronto: A Mentor Book, The New American Library, 1953)

Tykirm E, B, *Primitive Culture* (London: John Murray, 1871)

Van Rheenen, Gailyn *Communicating Christ in Animistic Contexts* (Grand Rapids, Mich.: Baker Book House, 1991)

Waddy, Charis, *The Muslim Mind* (London & New York: Longman Group Ltd., 1976)

Wahba, Sheikh Hafiz, *Arabian Days* (Arthur Narker Ltd., 1964)

Wehr, Hans, *A Dictionary of Modern Written Arabic*, Edited by J. Jilton Cowan, (Ithaca New York: Spoken Language Services, 1976)

Westernarck, E. A., *Pagan Survivals in Mohammedan Civilization* (London: Macmillan, 1933)

Zeid, Ahmend Abou, *Honor and Shame among the Bedouins of Egypt*, Honor and Shame: The Values of Mediterranean Society, (Chicago: University of Chicago Press, 1966) pp. 245-259

OTHER BOOKS BY ROLAND MULLER

The Man from Gadara

THE STORY OF ABDALLA HAWATMEH

Abdalla was born in the small village of Gadara, where long ago, Jesus cast the demons into swine. Growing up in a Muslim home, Abdalla often wondered about the religion he and his family practiced. When a scholarship opens the way for him to study in America, Abdalla renews his search for truth, and God. It is a long road, but God finally brings Abdalla to his knees before the cross.

Returning to the Middle East, Abdalla is led by God to start a ministry among the Muslims of his home country of Jordan. Eventually a group of believers is gathered, but can they withstand the pressure of the government, Muslim fanatics, and hostile Christians? Discover the amazing story of what God is doing in the Middle East through the Man from Gadara.

TOOLS FOR MUSLIM EVANGELISM

Just as every craftsman has his toolbox, evangelists should also have a box of tools ready for use when trying to explain the gospel to Muslims. Roland Muller introduces us to some of the tools and techniques used by successful evangelists in the Middle East. He also introduces us to the concept of 'teacher based evangelism' and demonstrates how it can be used in conjunction with or in place of friendship evangelism.

This book is rich in resources and practical wisdom drawn from many sources. The appendices include the Discover Lessons by Abdalla Hawatmeh, Literary and Audio-Visual Resources for Christians Sharing with Muslims by Ernest Hahn, excerpts from the digital resource 'Ministry Tools' and more.

Discover why this book is quickly becoming the evangelist's handbook for reaching Muslims with the gospel. Available from WEC International (Canada) and Essence Publishing. $14.95

MISSIONARY LEADERSHIP
by Motivation and Communication

Roland Muller

Illustrated by Jon Clime

How does one go about leading a team of missionary volunteers, drawn from a variety of cultures and denominations? In his new book, Roland Muller examines the differences between secular and biblical leadership, focusing in on the two main aspects of leading multi-cultural volunteer teams: motivation and communication.

This book includes a wealth of resources, worksheets, and more. It is illustrated with cartoons drawn by Jon Clime. A must for every missionary leader. $16.00 from Xlibris.

HAVE YOU READ THIS BOOK?

AVOIDING THE TENTMAKER TRAP
D. Gibson

Foreword by Patrick Johnstone

Is the tentmaker approach to missions biblical? Mr. Gibson, himself a tentmaker believes there is a strong biblical basis for tentmaking, but he also feels that the tentmaker approach to missions is fraught with dangers and difficulties for the uninitiated. Using his own experience, and the experiences of others, D. Gibson introduces us to a number of traps that have resulted in tentmakers returning home, disillusioned.

This book introduces two biblical methods of tentmaking, Pauline and Priscillan, and aids the reader in deciding which method he or she should take. It also includes a rich bibliography, and illustrations drawn from many countries around the world. Available from WEC International (Canada) $12.00

51668488R00070

Made in the USA
Lexington, KY
02 May 2016